Where the

Information Is

To Vera —
Happy e-mailing
Helen

71447.256
@CompuServe.
com

Where the Information Is

A Guide to Electronic Research for Nonprofit Organizations

by
Helen Bergan

BioGuide Press

Where the Information Is

A Guide to Electronic Research
for Nonprofit Organizations

by
Helen Bergan

BioGuide Press
P.O. Box 16072
Alexandria, VA 22302
(703) 820-9045

Publisher's Cataloging-in-Publication Data

Bergan, Helen J.
   Where the Information is: A Guide to Electronic Research for
   Nonprofit Organizations / Helen Bergan

p. cm.
Includes bibliographic references and index.
ISBN 0-9615277-2-2
1. Fund Raising 2. Nonprofit Organizations 3. Charities
4. Philanthropists 5. Internet (Computer Network) I. Title

   HG 177.B48   361.7   1996

Library of Congress Catalog Card Number 96-96139

Table of Contents

Preface

Everywhere you turn you see or hear about the electronic information superhighway. You are either interested, or you're not. If you do research for a nonprofit organization—for any reason—or wish to communicate with others in your field via e-mail or through bulletin boards, eventually you will have to become interested. The sooner the better.

The purpose of this book is to sort through the vast world of electronic information and determine what is available that will be of use, or of interest, to those in nonprofits. Although there will be an emphasis on prospect and donor research as part of the entire fund-raising process, the same techniques and computer equipment are useful for most types of research and communication.

In 1985, I wrote *Where the Money Is: A Fund Raiser's Guide to the Rich*. It mentioned online database searching with DIALOG and DataTimes, but mostly discussed print directories and indexes to biographical information. In 1992, I wrote the second edition of that book. It had a chapter entitled "Using Computers for Prospect Research." It discussed online searching and a few CD-ROM products. Besides that chapter, information on using electronics was scattered throughout the book. Still, the emphasis was on printed materials.

I would never discount using print materials for research. After all, as a reference librarian who spent most of my career before the electronics era, I value and treasure the old-fashioned book and its research value. Neither am I so old-fashioned that I am not astonished and delighted by the whiz-bang appeal of electronic research. I marvel at its speed, its ability to dig deeply into unrelated databases to ferret out minute details, and to present the information in print format, ready to be used for a multitude of purposes.

When I began to think about doing a third edition of *Where the Money Is*, I realized that the information in the 1992 edition was still very valid. The only part that had changed, and changed quickly, was the chapter on using computers for research. Reading that chapter now, it sounds a little dated. For beginners to computer research, it offers a hint of what is to come; now it is here. This book tells what's available and where to find it. The reasons to do prospect research and the benefits of it remain the same. Now, the difference is that prospect research can be done faster, better, and, in some cases, with less expense.

There are dozens of books with Internet in the title. Many others are about online research. I didn't read them all, but I did read enough books and enough journal articles to get the meat of what is now available that will be of interest to readers of this book. Most of the other books deal with online research in general. This will deal with online research for a specific group of users.

Throughout my research, for example, on the Internet, I kept thinking, "What's on it for me?" Much on the Internet is amazingly interesting. It can be a real time consumer. Its value for the type of research this book will cover is growing. It is a wonderful forum for like-minded folks to communicate and share information. Knowing how to access the Internet is of great value now to find some research material. It will continue to be even more important as more information becomes available on that network.

As I did research for this book, and wandered around online, it was tempting to think that everyone knows this already. That was because all I read was written by those who did know. Those who didn't know about electronic searching weren't writing about it or, perhaps, even talking about it. Some who don't yet use computers for research may have, perhaps, a bit of "compuphobia."

So, those of you who know all this book contains, let me congratulate you. I hope you will assist your colleagues who are not yet computer savvy. You may wish to read on to confirm that you are one of the insiders and way ahead of your nonprofit colleagues. Or, perhaps, you would prefer to sit down with a good mystery instead.

This book is for those with less self-confidence, those who know they should take advantage of all these electronic marvels, but don't know where to begin. They want a reference guide at their elbow. This book is for those who plan to, or are doing, some searching, perhaps on DIALOG. They may be stuck there and don't know about using consumer services such as CompuServe for economical searching. They may be scared to death—or at least intimidated—by any mention of the Internet. They may not know there are wonders on CD-ROMs available at their local academic or public libraries. This book is for them.

It's not an excuse, but it is reality. This book, and every other book on the subject of electronics, may be outdated before the print is dry. The information in it will still be true, but there will be other, newer, and more exciting products that should have been listed. If only they had existed while the book was being written. Throughout the book, and in the bibliography, there will be references to ongoing publications that give the newest information on new products as they become available.

Thanks to those who said there was a need for someone to bring all of this information together in book form, and encouraged me to write it. One colleague said it would be a daunting task. He was right.

My special thanks to Clarence Mundy, who drew the cartoons, and to Virginia Schmidt for her skillful editing. She also did the graphic design and book layout. Many friends offered ideas and encouragement. I appreciated their help.

While I was writing the book, names of products changed, companies were sold and merged, prices went up, and some even went down as the product became more popular and sold more copies. DIALOG Information Services, Inc., became Knight Ridder Information with DIALOG as one of many services. The American Prospect Research Association (APRA) became the Association of Professional Researchers for Advancement (still APRA).

Quick, get this book to the printer before anything else changes.

1

Introduction

*"Electric technology is forcing us to reconsider
and reevaluate practically every thought, every
action, and every institution formerly taken for
granted. Everything is changing...dramatically."*

Marshall McLuhan

No longer can we refer to the coming information age.
It's here. There is so much information around, the question is not what is available, but how to find it. Information must be in a usable form, either in print or electronic format, so those needing information can conveniently get it.

All kinds of nonprofit organizations, the small ones as well as the large ones, now can access the needed information with a minimum of electronic equipment, most already available in their offices.

Just what needs for information do most nonprofit organizations have? The basic need, of course, is where to get the funds necessary to keep the organization and its mission going. Call it what you want, fund raising or advancement, it keeps the nonprofit wheels turning. Knowing where to find those funds is needed information.

Only a few types of funding sources exist for nonprofits. That has not changed. There are foundation, corporation, and government grants. Then there are individual contributions. Sometimes they are through a private foundation, but finding information on the individual or the family that started the foundation is crucial to donation seeking.

For example, prospect research has been done for decades, though perhaps not called that. Gathering information on prospective wealthy donors has long been an accepted, necessary, process. With the marvels of electronics, the process, not the reason for it, has changed. For better, to be sure.

No longer need prospect researchers spend long hours in a university or public library searching for biographical and financial information. Authors, myself included, used to recommend using those public facilities to save money, rather than purchasing expensive directories that may or may not have the names researched. Now, much of that same information is available online. You pay for the minutes spent searching, not for the whole directory, using computer technology, accessed right there in the nonprofit office. Retrieved data is up-to-the-minute, as only online information can be.

Besides that basic need for funding, nonprofit offices need information on local businesses, demographic data, telephone numbers and addresses, management techniques, travel information, real estate values, and newspaper articles. The list could continue. The good news is that all such information is now easily available using modern electronics.

The history of electronics used by nonprofits follows that used in business. First there were mainframe computers. They were big, clumsy, and unreliable. They were used for storing information, but were not so good for retrieving it. Who can forget those "Do not staple, fold, or mutilate" punched cards? They were sorted by massive electronic dinosaurs.

Next there were personal computers, those desktop workstations, using floppy disks. For much of the day, the user switched floppies, each with different data on it. Then along came the hard disk, with its growing capacity. It made storage on floppy disks obsolete. But, there was still some worry. Would the hard disk fail? Return to the floppies for backup, just to be sure. Then came networks, so information stored and used by one office could be used by others within the organization.

Data to be stored had to be meticulously typed from carefully gathered data sheets. Most of what was stored was put together in-house, not retrieved from outside sources. Gradually a new term evolved. Information retrieval. It meant going elsewhere to find information. Once found, it could be stored for in-house use on your own computer system.

That is what we will discuss in this book. We will, mostly, skip the early years, as information went from book to electronic format. Hints about the future continue, but the current state of the art is dramatic enough. In a blink of the eye, you can get needed data from across the country—or across the world. From your desk, or from the computer in your home office, or the kid's bedroom computer, you can hook up with a world of information. It is there for a price, finally, that most can afford. Later chapters of this book will tell what resources are available online, and how to hook up to that much-praised "information superhighway."

Besides online resources, there is another format. It is, perhaps, even more exciting, and better for some kinds of research. It is the CD-ROM. These CD-ROMs are capable of storing an unfathomable amount of data on a 4.75-inch disk.

Print directories, thousands of pages long, can be contained on that small disk. Minute details can be found in a split second by the computer operator, using a CD-ROM drive. No more checking the index, paging back and forth to the wrong information, because it doesn't quite match. Now you can do Boolean (and/or/not) searching. Match up the criteria, push a key, and, wow, there it is. The next three chapters tell what is available on CD-ROMs for nonprofit organization research.

Realistically, most nonprofit organizations, doing any type of research, will use more than one of the new technologies. Some will decide to purchase a CD-ROM drive for office computers, some will decide they can get the best information through online research, others will use these technologies only at libraries.

Some will find that print resources are still useful and will use guides such as the second edition of *Where the Money Is* to find what information is where. Many decisions will depend on how much money and how many staff are doing research in any nonprofit organization and on whether there is a need to communicate with others around the country, or the world, through networks.

Lest readers think I am recommending all of these resources for purchase, let me assure you, I am not. There has been an attempt to evaluate the usefulness of each product for non-profits, and, especially, prospect research, purposes. But, this is by no means a complete directory of all that is available. The size of your organization and its fund-raising endeavors, plus the budget allocated, will determine what you can buy each year. Knowing these resources exist may be very useful. Also, what you purchase may depend on your proximity to a well-funded library and whether you are able to use the resources there.

Library funding has decreased recently, but in some cities there have been federal funds allocated for purchase of electronic resources. Don't be too surprised if your library, whether public or academic, does not have just the resource you want. If the library does not have the product on CD-ROM, for example, the librarian may suggest the possibility of getting the needed information online. Or, in the old-fashioned way, in a print reference book. This book discusses many of the same resources listed in *Where the Money Is*, but offers new ways to access the data. The emphasis is on CD-ROMs, online research through a variety of vendors, and the Internet, but it may also include some resources on floppy disks. It does not list or analyze electronic screening services unless they have research capabilities. Nor does it discuss data management software.

2

CD-ROMs: Lots of Information on a Small Disc

"The ever-whirling wheel of change"

Edmund Spenser, 1590

Perhaps, in this day of rapidly changing technology, one should not be surprised by what seems a miracle. That's how I feel about CD-ROMs. The little 4.75-inch plastic disc holds an encyclopedia. Really? And the vast amount of information is retrievable in a split second. Don't try to fool me, I thought. Impossible! Believe it, I was told. Now I believe, and I am a true believer in the miracle of CD-ROMs. Just don't ask me to explain it, but then don't ask me to explain computers either.

CD-ROMs were developed by two electronic companies, Sony and Phillips, around 1980. They have been commercially available since about 1986. The first CD-ROM I used — I think it was about 1989 — held the last several years of the *Washington Post* on one disc. With it, I could find reference to a single name, then retrieve the entire article, and print it out. Right there before my eyes. No more searching through printed newspaper indexes, hoping an article might include the name I searched for. No more tedious scrolling through microfilm. No more did I dread newspaper research. Now it was fun. I knew someone had paid a lot for the equipment and the CD-ROM, but I used it at a public library, so it cost me nothing. Amazing. What would they think of next?

During the years since then, publishers have thought of many other reference resources that lend themselves to this electronic medium. To name a few besides full-text newspapers: phone directories for the whole country, business directories and SEC reports, ZIP code directories, encyclopedias (with motion and sound), full-text back issues of magazines, criss-cross telephone and address directories, language instruction, college directories, everything you want to know about dinosaurs, guides to grants, a tour of the National Gallery in London, unabridged dictionaries, directories of foundations, every kind of sports games, and, horrors, the H.R. Haldeman diaries on CD-ROM so you can wallow forever in Watergate, if you think you must.

The initials CD-ROM stand for Compact Disc-Read Only Memory. In short, that means information is on a disc that looks just like the kind you play on your music compact disc player. Instead of music, it holds digital data. Lots of it. To compare, one floppy disk holds about one megabyte of data. A CD-ROM holds more than 600-700 megabytes—thus more than 600 floppies. The equivalent of more than 300,000 pages of text or 650 reams of paper. Or a stack of pages 135 feet high.

If you were to transmit enough data to fill a single CD-ROM at 2,400 bauds per second, it would take 23 days. All on that thin plastic disc you can hold in the palm of your hand. (As it used to be with how long it took to get to the moon, the comparable numbers vary, depending on who gives them.)

Already multimedia producers are planning for the future. One possibility is a disc with data sandwiched between layers, to be read one layer at a time, by laser beams. The potential? Up to a million pages per disc.

Production costs for a CD-ROM are going down, as are the drives to play them on. It costs much less to produce a master CD-ROM, going down from a high of $2,000. After that, each additional single disc can cost just a few dollars. Much less than to print a book. As more CD readers are available, more publishers will be putting their works into this medium. Then, prices will do down further. Worldwide, it has been estimated there are 47 million CD-ROM players in use at the end of 1995. By the end of this century, 80 percent of computer users will have CD-ROM drives attached to their systems.

The ROM part means that you can read from the disc, but you cannot edit or add anything to it. That is part of its value. The discs, just like music ones, are difficult to ruin. You can't erase it by mistake.

Easier than discussing how big is a byte, just realize that an entire 20-volume encyclopedia fits on one disc. Or, if you understand this better, the entire *Random House Unabridged Dictionary* (all 13 pounds and 8-inches thick) goes on one disc. With bytes to spare.

Besides the amazing size, or lack of it, of a CD-ROM, is the equally amazing accessibility of information on it. Using that *Random House Unabridged Dictionary* as an example, you can, of course, find the meanings of words by typing in the word. The entry is displayed on the screen. But, you say, you don't know how to spell the word. What then? Type in what you know, putting a question mark where you are unsure, and the word, or a choice of matching words, is displayed. If you are really unsure, there is a browse function. A box pops up and you type in a few letters and a list of words is displayed.

Continuing with the dictionary example, to show the diversity of CD-ROM searching, you can hunt for a word, if you know its definition, as each word of the definition is searchable. You're looking for the name of a French painter, and know you would recognize it if you saw it, you can type in "French AND painter," and the screen gives you a list of all that fit that description. The word AND, in caps, means search for those two words in the definition in the entire dictionary. Faster than you can say Claude Monet. Or, if you are sure you don't want an impressionist, type in "French AND painter NOT impressionist."

The marvels go on. The CD-ROM *Random House Unabridged Dictionary* speaks! Each of its 315,000 entries is pronounced by a human voice and is audible on multimedia personal computers. Both men's and women's voices. Equal opportunity, and chosen without regional accents. Using a CD-ROM dictionary can be more fun than many computer games.

Encyclopedias on CD-ROM have been around for many years. Their publishers realized that by adding motion videos and sound, now possible on a compact disc, they could enhance the pictures and words of the print encyclopedias. Instead of a whole set of books, you get one disc. You spend less, and get more for your money. In fact, beginning in 1993, CD-ROM encyclopedias sold more than printed ones. Why not. They don't take shelf space or need to be dusted.

Sure, your nonprofit office can get along with a print dictionary (especially now that your word processor has a spell checker) and you don't need an encyclopedia there, but wouldn't it be nice to have one? Before I tell you which CD-ROM products you just might need, let me give you a few details about what equipment you will need to use them.

If you are planning to upgrade your office (or home) personal computer, seriously consider getting a complete multimedia personal computer system that comes with a CD-ROM drive, a sound card, and speakers. Prices are going down as demand increases. Go to your local computer store or call one of many mail-order computer companies, and discuss your needs. Tell what you want the computer to do and listen to the recommendations. System requirements for most of the CD-ROM products mentioned in this book are similar, depending on whether you use an IBM/IBM compatible or Macintosh system.

"Software consultant, 40 hrs/wk, $53,000/yr. Supervise analysts and programmers. Requires 6 yrs. of high school."

ComputerWorld (*PC Magazine*, Sept. 13, 1994)

CD-ROMs: Lots of Information on a Small Disc

You will need at least a 386 PC, but a 486 or Pentium is better, a high-resolution color monitor, at least 8 megabytes of memory, and a quadruple-speed CD-ROM drive with a Sound Blaster compatible card. (Dual-speed drives are okay, but you might as well be ahead of the crowd.)

Aside from a quick way to access information, CD-ROMs are very useful for office or business applications. Communications, presentations, and research can be more dynamic with multimedia features such as sound, video, and even animation, made possible with CD-ROMs.

Besides all the reference products available, many software publishers prefer to distribute their new products and upgrades on a CD-ROM, instead of on 10 to 15 high-density disks as many graphic intensive programs require. This makes loading software from a CD-ROM easier than inserting many floppy disks as the program loads. Because of the massive amount of data able to be stored on this media, software on a CD-ROM can include abundant help information.

Many word processing programs now come with the actual word processing program and also an unabridged dictionary, a thesaurus, a quotation book, a world almanac, and an encyclo-pedia—all on a single CD-ROM.

Each day there are more and more reasons to join the CD-ROM world. If that is true for home computer buyers, it is surely even more true for office/business computer buyers. Any discussion of where the information is must emphasize that a lot of it is on CD-ROM. Those computer experts who were slow realizing how fast this field was going to develop are now saying that information CD-ROMs will be around a long time. No longer is a multimedia system just for fun and games.

Following are some CD-ROMs on a variety of topics that can be very useful for nonprofit offices. Some are rather inex-pensive and most are available at software computer shops and office supply stores, often at discount prices. As with most computer products, look around for the best prices on CD-ROMs.

ENCYCLOPEDIAS

Encyclopedias on CD-ROMs are one of the best bargains around. Most cost around $50 and are available in computer stores.

Grolier Multimedia Encyclopedia. Based on the popular 21-volume *Academic American Encyclopedia*, this disc has 10 million words of text, plus charts, photos, and illustrations, many in color. With six hours of multimedia sequences, it offers what no print volumes can—the sounds of history as it was made.

Microsoft Encarta 96 Encyclopedia is the first CD-ROM encyclopedia to take real advantage of online possibilities. Its earlier versions pioneered multimedia with many hours of audio and video clips. You could hear bits of your favorite composer's works, see full-color pictures from the world's leading art galleries, and hear cries from the animal kingdom.

Now, beginning with the 1996 edition, Encarta offers online updates from Microsoft's home page on the World Wide Web at its address (http://www.microsoft.com/Encarta) or through the company's Microsoft Network services. This Yearbook Builder feature allows users to get monthly updates so, as the world changes, you can keep informed. Downloading takes about 10 minutes with a 14,400-baud modem. It's free until August 1996, then there will be a subscription fee.

DICTIONARIES

Here's the ultimate. The *Oxford English Dictionary.* It's better than the original 2nd edition of the printed 20-volume work by the same name. It includes the same 616,500 words, to be sure, but makes searching for them much easier with easy cross-referencing, Boolean (and/or/not) searches, and a powerful search engine that lets you gather what you need in ways you can't in a print dictionary. Okay, I never said it was cheap. At $895, you will need to have an office full of word lovers and a gift from Santa Claus to convince yourself it is needed. If so, call Oxford University Press at 1-800-451-7556.

Consider this one instead. The *Random House Unabridged Dictionary.* It is the speaking dictionary mentioned earlier. It has about half the words of the *Oxford* because it doesn't include obsolete terms and expressions, (but you probably shouldn't be using them anyway.) It is American English, it is easier to use, and is available from Random House Reference and Electronic Publishing at 1-800-733-3000. It's $70, or $100 if you want a print copy also. But, why would you? It doesn't speak.

OFFICE SOFTWARE

Microsoft Bookshelf combines many reference sources into one linked tool. The popular one-volume *Concise Columbia Encyclopedia* is here, along with the *Hammond Intermediate World Atlas,* the *World Almanac and Book of Facts, American Heritage Dictionary, The People's Chronology, Roget's Original Thesaurus,* and the *Columbia Dictionary of Quotations.*

Beginning with the 1995 version, it includes a handy ZIP code locating tool. Consider the quotations dictionary essential for speakers or writers who wish to slip in words of the masters to enhance their own authority on any subject; $99 from Microsoft Corporation at 1-800-426-9400 or discounted at computer shops.

If you do any type of publishing, either in-house or with newsletters, consider *Corel Gallery.* While there is a lot of clip-art around in various software packages that may fill up your hard disk with useless outdated nostalgia pieces, graphics are better on a CD-ROM. You won't have to shuffle through a lot of floppies to find the bit of art you want, because it's all on a compact disc. This has 10,000 nice clips, most in color, with a printed directory of all images so they can be easily retrieved. It has keyword searching, easy drag-and-drop features and a thumbnail viewer. For less than $50, you'll be tempted to put some zip into your routine memos around the office. Call Corel Corporation at 1-800-836-3729.

MAPS AND TRAVEL PLANNERS

Street Atlas USA. This is great fun to use and a great conversation piece. If you need to go somewhere and don't have a paper map, it can get you there. Before sending development officers out on those trips to prospects, make sure they know the way.

With *Street Atlas USA*, you can find locations by address, ZIP code, or telephone area code, but try zooming in on your desired location. Start out with a seamless map of the whole country, then zoom in until you get down to the desired street. With over 12 million streets included, it's easy. You can print out maps of any area you choose, at a variety of magnifications. Just to illustrate the amazing effect of CD-ROMs, if you were to print out all of *Street Atlas USA*, at the highest magnification, the finished map would cover more than 10 football fields. All on one skinny disc! About $75 from DeLorme, a mapping company, in Freeport, Maine.

DeLorme also does *Global Explorer*, a detailed world atlas on CD-ROM, for $69, and *Map'n'Go* at $29. Whether you're planning a convention, a retreat, or just a weekend away from the office, consider this product. Decide where you want to go, type in the destination and a few details about your preferences, and this product will get you there with no trouble. You can print out the best routes with a listing of accommodations and sights along the way. Call DeLorme at 1-800-452-5931 or 1-207-865-9291 for information or to order.

There's only one problem with many of these CD-ROM products. They are so much fun they may cut down office productivity. No matter that you bought the above product to help get you to regional meetings the quickest way (or whatever the excuse to buy it), it will be used by every staff member planning a vacation or an upcoming long weekend.

Rand McNally has a product called *TripMaker*. It started out as a floppy disk for PCs running Windows and then went to one CD-ROM. It's designed to help those planning trips by car. Tell it where you want to go, and *TripMaker* does the rest. It suggests either scenic or direct routes, calculates mileage and travel time, provides information on tolls, and estimates costs for lodging and gas. It suggests journeys based on scenic, historic, entertainment, or other points of interest—with sound and video. It's also good for armchair travelers. Look for it where maps are sold and at computer stores for about $40.

TAXI is a CD-ROM travel guide to cities. It lists hotels, restaurants, and cultural attractions. Best of all, it gives the best route to those places from your hotel, and tells how far away they are. This, of course, implies you have your very own CD-ROM drive on your portable computer and it is always with you when you go off to a convention or to visit donors in other cities. Better yet, do the research before you leave your own office. It's from the Middlegate Company of Clinton, New Jersey, at 1-800-439-8294 (that translates into HEY TAXI). Regional CD-ROMs cover five cities for $59.95; a national edition for twenty cities is $159.95.

GENEALOGY

Whether you are researching your own genealogy or trying to document the family histories of your major donors, *Family Tree Maker* can help. It is a CD-ROM product that includes much more than just diagrams on which to place names. This gives access to names themselves. Over 100 million of them, taken from a wide variety of indexes. Check the index for ancestral names, then if the names are found, further indexes can be ordered from a research company in Utah, affiliated with the Mormon archives. No longer must you take a trip to one of those very complete Mormon genealogy libraries to get a family history started. *Family Tree Maker* on CD-ROM for Windows is from Banner Blue Software, Inc., in Fremont, California. Look for it at computer software chain stores for around $60, or call 1-510-794-6850.

TELEPHONE AND ADDRESS DIRECTORIES

Do you remember when you had to call a long-distance operator to get an out-of-town phone number? That wasn't bad, but then the long-distance companies started charging, sometimes 75 cents a pop, for the service. The amount, month by month, added up. You could call or go to a public library that had a large collection of other-city phone books, or use a product called "Phone Fiche," which was a collection of phone books on microfiche. Nothing worked very well.

Then along came CD-ROM technology, and it was as if made for a national phone directory. It didn't take long for such a product to be produced. In fact, it was one of the first inexpensive reference CD-ROMs made, coming out in 1986. Several companies now have CD-ROM phone books.

All the phone numbers in the country combined on compact discs? Incredible, but true. (Well, almost.) And, best of all, you can search many ways. A donor has moved, but you don't know where. Try a name search—but it's tricky if the name is not an unusual one. You will get a country seemingly filled with John Petersons. If you can narrow down a state or, better, a city, you'll have better luck and save time.

Save money and check a CD-ROM phone book before you call the distant area code's 555-1212 information number. Check those addresses before you send out the Christmas cards (to say nothing about your fund-raising letters.) You'll save money on returned mail, and more of your letters will go where intended.

Beware. Nothing is perfect. Neither are these phone directories on CD-ROM. As you know, persons and families in this country relocate often, so keeping any directory up to date is impossible. *PC Computing* magazine (July 1995) estimated that phone directories on CD-ROM are about 60 percent accurate, and not all phone directories in the country are included. Whatever the current accuracy rate, it will continue to improve.

PhoneDisc suggests there are better ways to find a number than letting your fingers do the walking. That may work for finding local associates, but forget it for cross-country travel. You need something better, and *PhoneDisc* has it. All residential numbers (about 81 million) are on two discs, one for the western and the second for the eastern states, at $79. It retrieves names, phone numbers, addresses, and ZIP codes. Another, also $79, covers over 9.5 million business phones, addresses, business type, or SIC code on one disc for the country, with the capability for reverse searching.

The Combo Pack combines the business and residential sets. PowerFinder combines both sets with reverse search indexing (by name, business type, and SIC code) for about $100. Phone numbers and addresses (with ZIP codes not found in phone directories) are included. Persons with unlisted numbers won't be there, nor will others who have somehow escaped the tentacles of direct-mail advertisers, so up to 15 percent of the country may be missed. The data is updated quarterly with information from phone companies or by scanning or keying every page from the country's 4,800 phone books.

The data supplier uses huge mainframe computers to add ZIP codes and standardize city and street names. It sends the data through the Postal Service Change of Address File (PCOA) to pick up those changes. The end result is an easy-to-use tool for unlimited phone number and address searching. For details on *PhoneDisc* call Digital Directory Assistance at 1-800-284-8353 or 1-301-657-8548.

Select Phone offers unlimited downloading from its 80 million listings so it is often preferred over those that limit downloading. This has an interesting feature. It has the usual searching capacity by name, city, ZIP codes, and even SIC codes for businesses. With its companion software package, called *MapView* for Windows, you can export found listings to a U.S. map to see where your best prospects are clustered. This is useful when you think the searched-for person lives "somewhere around Chicago." The list price, including *MapView* for Windows, is $119, but check the street price. Call Pro CD at 1-800-992-3766 or 1-508-750-0055 for details.

A stand-alone software system called *MapLinx* can take information from a data management database or spreadsheet and put them on a map within a ZIP, area code, county, or city. Putting facts into interactive maps, *MapLinx* can group your prospects and donors by area. For example, if a member of your staff plans to visit a city, it can tell which persons from your data list live close by. It costs $99.95 and is available at computer stores.

For details, call MapLinx Corporation at 1-800-308-5359 or 1-214-231-1400.

American White Pages, on CD-ROM, includes 70 million consumers. Information can be selected by name, length of residence, and median home value. It can be used for verifying information or just looking for numbers for nonprofit donors, friends, and prospects. It's $49, available from American Business Information at 1-800-555-5666 or 1-402-593-4595.

American Business Information does several other telephone directories on CD-ROM at very reasonable prices. Among those are the *11 Million Businesses Phone Book,* the *American Yellow Pages, 800 Number Phone Book, 70 Million Households Phone Book,* and the *9-Digit Zip-Code Directory.*

Keep in mind there are many ways to get telephone information for individuals or businesses. In early 1996, this company began offering its business database on America Online. Other similar files are on CompuServe and the Internet.

Some copy-writers for these CD-ROM products get a bit carried away. For example:

"Picture a Phonebook on steroids. If you think of this CD-ROM as mere telephone listings in another format, you've only one toe in the water. Its search and retrieval powers alone make it more akin to the radar screen on a nuclear submarine."

Okay. Stop!

CD-ROMs: Lots of Information on a Small Disc

MetroSearch Digital Database from Metromail at R.R. Donnelley & Sons Company offers a CD-ROM cross-reference directory of 100 million listings for the country. Or you can get just your own region, from a set of 10 regional directories. You can search by name, address, city, or any combination, including how long one has been at that address. If you know the phone number, use that. It is based on ZIP code data, so includes median income and median housing values. High-income neighborhoods can be selected.

Metromail has a look-up service that will search for people nationwide, for a price, of course. You supply the name and as much defining information as possible, and they will give you the details, plus the demographic data for the area of the address. That is based on a wealth rating, depending on the area, so it differs by state.

This service uses a 900 number at $3 for the first minute and $2 every minute after, charged to your telephone bill. Another option is a low-volume monthly subscription at $17.50 plus $1.75 per search with additional charges, depending on depth of the search, up to $15 per search for the entire country. A high-volume option costs $500 per month. Call 1-800-228-4571 for this search service or, interestingly, to get yourself off their mailing lists. By paying per search you can see how helpful the whole CD-ROM may be.

Prices for the CD-ROM product vary from a hundred to several thousand dollars per year, depending on regions and update cycles selected. Call 1-800-793-2536 or 1-800-638-7623.

Metromail is a distributor of rented mailing lists provided to commercial companies and nonprofit organizations. As such, this company and others providing lists are concerned about the privacy issue. As more information is available on persons, there is a growing concern that it is overused or used for the wrong purposes. As direct marketers hope to reach the maximum number of interested persons for their products, while eliminating others, the idea of "ethnicated" lists became available, causing concern as persons were put into ethnic slots based on name alone.

ZIP CODE DIRECTORIES

9-DIGIT ZIP CODE DIRECTORY is from American Business Information, Inc. You can use the bulky 2-volume print ZIP directory available from the U.S. Postal Service, or you can use one CD-ROM disc instead. The computerized version is faster and more fun, and only $29. As with the other directories, just type in the street address and the ZIP code appears on the screen. Or, you can find out where in the country the ZIP code is located. Call 1-402-593-4600.

Another, with the clever name of *USA UNZIPPED*, lets you instantly verify any address in the United States. Nine-digit codes are given, down to the precise apartment number, with easy-to-use techniques. Although there are programs that can add the extended digits to your complete mailing list, this is useful for checking individual ZIP codes or for getting the extensions, thus helping the Postal Service deliver your mail.

This disc contains 30 million households and 1 million business addresses. Type in city and state (or select it from the listing), then pick street name and address range from pull-down menus that automatically appear. These addresses can be transferred through most word processing or mailing list programs. It's $49.95 from CD LIGHT in Sandy, Utah, at 1-800-571-3914. It is also available as a floppy disk (5-digit ZIPs only) for $29.95 for those without a CD-ROM drive.

CD LIGHT has a support forum on CompuServe. If you have a CompuServe membership, just type GO CD LIGHT and look for a catalog of products plus information on the U.S. Postal Service, including rates and locations of USPS Business Centers. As changes are made in bulk mail rules and rates, CD LIGHT will keep you informed in this support forum.

If you don't have a CD-ROM drive (but are still reading this chapter) consider *ZipZapp*, a similar program available for DOS, Windows, and Macintosh. It allows the user to look up a ZIP code while in another software application, such as a word processor. A telephone area code search makes it possible to see where you are calling, before you return that long distance call. Call True Basic at 1-800-436-2111 or 1-603-298-8517.

DIRECTORIES OF CD-ROMS

So how do you keep track of what is available now, or coming soon, on this relatively new research tool? Sure enough, there is a directory available from Information Today, Inc. Their *CD-ROM Finder* is in book format, at $69.50. It lists more than 2,000 titles with their hardware requirements. It will help you find the right discs for your precise needs. The current sixth edition is 40 percent larger than the fifth edition, showing how the technology is growing. Call 1-609-654-6266 or look for the directory at an academic or public library.

CD-ROMs in Print does for this technology what *Books in Print* does for print volumes. If you are researching an obscure subject and wonder if it is on CD-ROM, check here. Originally from Mecklermedia, the 8th edition is now from Gale Research, Inc. It includes 1,300 new entries, at approximately $130. Call 1-800-877-4253.

3

CD-ROMs: Consider These for the Nonprofit Office

"We all need to work toward doing our jobs more efficiently. To that end, much of the new technology (CD-ROMs, online databases, etc.) should help, if only we knew how to use these new resources with the same ease as we use our trusty old directories."

APRA member

The next CD-ROMs are those more or less important for your nonprofit office, depending on the type of research you do. Some of these CD-ROMs may be just what you need for in-house purchase because you will use them so often. In 1994 the American Prospect Research Association, as it was then called, surveyed its members and found 28.6 percent used CD-ROMs in their research offices.

You may not be shocked by the price of some of these products, as others in small development offices may be. For those in large university development offices, for example, these CD-ROMs may already be available for everyday use. For others, they may be considered wished-for items.

If you are considering purchasing any of these, my advice is to call around to close-by public or academic libraries. Ask if the product you are interested in is available there. Unless you live near a well-funded, large public library, you may have better luck calling a large academic library. If they have what you want, ask if there are any restrictions about who can use the library. Use the product at a library, if possible, and analyze its usefulness for your office.

Remember also, many of these databases are available online. That may get what you need with less up-front cost. Online, you purchase just the tidbits of information you need, as you need them. For small offices, that may be a better option.

One useful resource, from Gale Research, Inc., is the *Encyclopedia of Associations: National Organizations of the U.S. (CD-ROM)*. Instead of the 13 print volumes, you get it all on one compact disc. It includes 23,000 national organizations in the United States; 13,000 international and multinational organizations; and 54,000 regional, state, and local organizations. With the search capabilities of a CD-ROM, the user can research data by subject or keyword, association name, or geographic area. Or the researcher can combine elements for a more complex search.

Searching the *Encyclopedia of Associations* can identify individuals in association positions, organizations that can be of use for a host of different purposes, and mailing lists of value. If you want to know if a professional directory for an association exists, check this resource. As you browse, you'll be amazed at the number of associations that exist, some perfectly complementing the needs of your charitable organization. It is also a good way to see if there is a local or regional chapter in your area. It includes an executive index and can be searched using Boolean logic, enabling the user to retrieve information as precisely defined. The multivolume print set is available in most libraries; many will now have the CD-ROM version that costs $595. Call 1-800-877-GALE.

If you plan to do a lot of online searching and need to identify some obscure databases, the *Gale Directory of Databases CD-ROM* offers the most complete and convenient coverage available anywhere. The January 1995 edition lists

9,385 databases, 3,400 producers, 825 online services, and 990 vendors/distributors. The numbers grow by leaps and bounds each year.

A brief description and contact information are given for each database, including those available through which online vendors or available on CD-ROM; it costs $600. Call 1-800-877-GALE.

Those are two examples of general reference value. But what CD-ROM products will be most useful for your nonprofit office? No matter how intrigued you are by the electronic products in the previous chapter, here are some CD-ROM products of special value to nonprofit offices.

Unfortunately, these products are not as inexpensive as those with more wide-spread commercial and home use. Contact each company for current prices, as sometimes there are special offers available. Ask specific questions, outlining what you need. Ask if the CD-ROM gives that information.

CORPORATE INFORMATION

Since the electronic era, retrieving information on corporations has become easier. Beginning in 1996, all public companies must file their annual reports electronically. Because most have already done that, along with all Securities and Exchange Commission-required reports, it is now easier for the SEC to disseminate that information.

Many nonprofit development offices have long used *Disclosure* online through DIALOG. Since 1968, when the company was founded to provide timely and accurate information on publicly traded companies, *Disclosure* has retrieved and sold documents and computerized synopses of documents filed with the SEC. It covers virtually all public companies in the United States, approximately 15,000 in all. The *Disclosure SEC Database* gives both current and historical financial data; directory information such as corporate addresses, officers, and directors; plus management information regarding corporate goals, major activities, and such.

For your fund-raising purposes, financial data from the 10-K and the proxy statements are very useful. The 10-K annual business and financial report needs to be filed with the SEC within 90 days after the fiscal year end. Comparing the last few years for the company, you can get a picture of its status. The proxy statement is an annual document, listing directors and key stock ownership information. Both give salaries and other remuneration figures. Some proxies give biographical information such as age and membership on other corporate and nonprofit boards. These are clues to your prospect's interests.

As a fund-raising example, with this CD-ROM product, a college or university researcher could check for graduates of that institution who have important corporate positions. If the school was mentioned in the biographical sketch, a search will find it, and a list can be compiled.

It is important to understand ownership terminology as it relates to SEC requirements. "Five Percent Owners" are those individuals, companies, banks, or funds that own at least five percent of the company's shares. (SEC began to require these five percenters to file just a few years ago.) "Inside Owners" consist of officers, beneficial owners, and principal stockholders owning ten percent or more of a company's stocks. Officers, directors, and beneficial owners must hold at least 1,000 shares to be included.

With a very few exceptions, all this corporate information is on CD-ROM as *Compact D/SEC*. It's the best of all worlds. You get volumes of data on a single disc, plus incredibly fast response at your own computer, at any time, around the clock. But for a hefty price, of course.

Disclosure/Worldscope gives ten years of financial information for companies in 40 countries and in 24 major industries, useful as your international corporate information needs expand.

For some of you, because you do heavy-duty corporate research as part of your corporate philanthropy needs, you may wish to subscribe to your own *Disclosure* on CD-ROM. Others may be able to find it at a library with a good business reference section. Perhaps the best place to find *Disclosure* is at your college or university library. Indeed, the company marketing suggests its use for undergraduate and graduate research, if the university or college offers business degrees. Use it for your corporate and individual fund-raising prospecting. (If you are connected to that academic institution, you might explore networking possibilities with the library. That adds to the original cost, but makes it available in more sites, depending on licensing.)

Some of you will need only bits and pieces of the information on this huge database and will find it economical to get *Disclosure* information online through DIALOG or Compu Serve. Beware, in most cases, corporate information is the most costly of all online information.

Call *Disclosure* at 1-800-846-0365 or 1-800-843-7747 for current prices.

Standard & Poor's Register of Corporations, Directors, and Executives, long a favorite for any type of corporate research, on CD-ROM is more user friendly than its print version. You can do keyword searches for the entire text. For example, knowing an individual's name, you can find all "hits" for that person, including outside directorships. This is a strong product for nonprofit researchers because it gives brief personal information on 70,000 executives, not just business affiliation. It includes date and place of birth, education (where and how much), and corporate and fraternal memberships.

Although the CD-ROM version (available first in 1995) costs $995, compared to $625 for the print volumes, it will soon become the preferred way to get corporate information. You can hold the data in the palm of your hand, something you cannot do with the print volumes. With CD-ROM you can get a print copy of needed information without lugging those huge volumes to the copy machine. It is also available in a "direct marketing" version with label-making capability.

Call S&P at 1-212-208-8786.

Knight-Ridder Information OnDisc offers *Standard & Poor's Corporations* including S&P Public Companies, S&P Private Companies, and S&P Executives. The product is searchable by numerous fields. It's $4,900 for an annual subscription with monthly CD-ROM updates. Call 1-800-343-2564.

Walker's Corporate Directory on CD-ROM gives data on the top 10,000 publicly traded U.S. companies. It takes summary business and financial information from the annual report, proxy, and 10-K reports and gives a good picture of a company's operation. That includes executives, stock holdings by officers, sales and net income, ticker symbol, stock prices and dividend return.

The CD-ROM comes with easy-to-use search software; it is menu driven and quick. You can locate and download information or make mailing lists from companies you select.

The 1995 CD-ROM edition costs $595. Call Walker's Western Research at 1-800-258-5737.

As Gale Research Inc. was a major player producing reference books for library and other markets since the 60s, now they are producing CD-ROM tools at a fast clip. *Ward's Business Directory* (the data is compiled by Information Access Company) and the *World Trade Centers Association World Business Directory* are combined on one CD-ROM called *Companies International* that gives quick access to information on nearly a quarter million companies located in the United States and 180 countries abroad.

All of the basic business information is here with the exception of company executives and directors. Companies can be searched in a variety of ways: by geography—city, state, ZIP code, area code, or country; company size—by sales volume, number of employees; or type of industry by specific SIC 4-digit codes. A single-user version costs $1,995. Call Gale at 1-800-877-GALE.

Ward's Business Directory also is available online, in Company Intelligence, File 479 on DIALOG. This may be the most economical way to get needed business data. With your modem you can dial into the database, and probably get all you need for much less than buying the complete CD-ROM.

Another idea, if you need just location information is to use phone directories on CD-ROM as listed in the previous chapter.

Because it is sometimes hard to discover the key persons in local businesses, *Contacts Influential* can help. It is another service from American Business Information, Inc., available as print or diskette directories for many metropolitan areas. This names top decision makers for each company and gives other company data. They are priced between $215 and $345 for these cities or areas: Seattle, Tacoma/Olympia, Portland, Willamette, San Diego, Denver, Colorado Front Range, Minneapolis, St. Paul, Kansas City, Tampa/St. Petersburg, and Orlando. Call Contacts Influential at 1-612-672-9974.

An old reliable reference source in book format is the *Directory of Corporate Affiliations*. Rather than the six-volume set, it is online through DIALOG, or on CD-ROM as *Corporate Affiliations Plus* from Reed Reference Publishing at 1-800-521-8110. Knowing the "ancestry" of private and public companies is very helpful in determining if the company you research is owned elsewhere. This gives the company's "family tree" and business financial reports, plus names and titles of top executives. It costs around $2,000. Call 1-800-521-8110.

Much data on companies was originally compiled for credit purposes. One of the oldest companies, Dun & Bradstreet, offers financial statements and payment histories for 9.3 million companies. *Dun & Bradstreet Information Services* is available on CD-ROM, online, or by phone.

One of the most used source of prospect research on corporations and their executives has long been the *Dun & Bradstreet Million Dollar Directory*. Now on CD-ROM, it's called *Dun's Million Dollar Disc*. This lists those companies with net worth over $500,000, with biographical data on almost half-a-million top executives. It's $3,900.

Call 1-800-255-9220 for Dun & Bradstreet products.

Hoover's Masterlist of Major U.S. Companies may be useful for quick identification of about 6,000 companies. Information given is mostly directory data and, on CD-ROM, it is just $99.95 from The Reference Press at 1-800-486-8666. Or try it online with CompuServe, there called *Hoover's Company Database* as "Company Profiles," with detailed company information, or "Company Capsules," with just a brief synopsis. Online you pay just for what you need.

DUN & BRADSTREET'S MARKETPLACE DIRECTORY features 10 million business addresses, rather than individuals, for fast look-up. It is a companion volume to *D&B MARKETPLACE*. Both include mailing addresses, SIC codes, executive names, and company size. The *Directory* can be used when you want to quickly check a few specific companies by name. Use *MarketPlace* when you want to build a list of companies. It allows users to become their own list broker of business prospects by defining the desired companies, then making labels or reports from those items chosen. For example, you may wish to target specific businesses in your metropolitan area or state for attention. With this database you can pick and choose addresses from the list. You are not confined to whatever a list broker may send.

This product uses a software meter, refillable by phone, presumably by credit card, to keep track of what data is retrieved or printed as labels. Unlike labels from list brokers, you can use the database for additional labels for one year, metered by use.

Both CD-ROMs cost $849 but may be discounted from MarketPlace Information Corp. at 1-800-590-0065. That includes the ability to "unlock" up to $300 worth of data from the CD-ROM (equivalent to mailing list information on 3,000 companies.)

American Yellow Pages is, as it sounds, just that. Compiled by American Business Information, it lists over 10 million U.S. businesses, divided by 7,000 yellow page headings and/

or SIC codes. It gets information from more than 5,000 telephone directories, corporate reports, SEC 10-K reports, state and chamber of commerce directories, and other public sources to compile this CD-ROM directory. The database is searchable by firm name, business owner or CEO, type, area, or telephone area code. Call for details at 1-800-555-5666 or 1-402-593-4565. For a mere $69, it may give you just enough location information.

These directories may be useful for compiling mailing labels, but some have download limits and licensing restrictions that prohibit you from using them for business or marketing purposes. When you ask for information from the company before deciding which will work for you, ask about downloading. Though basically the same, some offer different features and allow a different number of downloads. If you use a phone directory of companies to help compile a mailing list, consider sending your mailings to specific ZIP codes in your city, or mail to the entire city. It's possible with some of the new address directories on CD-ROM and other new technologies.

It is a good idea to check around in your own community for lists of local businesses. Some are available on floppy diskette for little cost. Check with your local economic development office or the chamber of commerce, or ask at the public library for available resources for your area. Many public libraries collect annual reports for local companies.

DIRECTORY OF BOARD MEMBERS

BoardLink—The Essential Networking Tool for Nonprofits on CD-ROM from Taft Group includes over 130,000 board members of the largest 1,000 corporations, 5,000 nonprofit organizations, and 6,000 philanthropic foundations. It's a "who knows whom" publication, designed for networking between directors of boards. The theory is, of course, that knowing others on influential corporate and nonprofit boards gives the proverbial "foot in the door" with that person. It even may be the person's home door. Home addresses, or another contact address of more than 50,000 board members, are given.

Listings are arranged in two indexes, alphabetically by organizations' and directors' names, compiled from business and organization documents. The CD-ROM edition costs around $1,000 and is also available on diskettes. Call 1-800-877-8238.

For the affluent nonprofit organization, **Boardlink Plus!** offers the chance to make connections between influential board members of corporations, foundations, and nonprofit organizations. It takes data from IRS 990 and 990-PF filings and from SEC documents. Extended biographical profiles from proxy statements are included for more than 15,000 corporate directors. Call Taft or Gale Research for pricing.

Directory of Directors, from Waltman Associates, is available on disk or as a bound book for specific cities, listing those

prominent individuals on coprorate and nonprofit boards. The following cities or states are available: Atlanta, California, Dallas-Fort Worth, Denver, Houston, Portland, Seattle-Tacoma, and the Twin Cities. A directory for each city, in either format, costs $195.

National Directory of College and University Trustees is from Waltman Associates and provides over 50,000 names with occupation and address. It covers four-year colleges and universities, both public and private, in the United States, Canada, and Mexico. It costs $195. Call 1-612-338-0772 for additional information or to order.

DEMOGRAPHIC DATA

If you're planning ahead to the turn of the century, look for future demographic data in *The Sourcebook of ZIP Code Demographics* from CACI Marketing Systems. It gives household type, income range, race, population, and marketing potential for each ZIP code in the country, with five-year projections. It's in book format, but also on diskettes and a very accessible CD-ROM. Any nonprofit organization doing mass mailings will want to know the demographics of the area before purchasing lists, for example. Just as businesses use demographic research before opening a store, or expanding into a neighborhood, so nonprofits can use this same information as they plan their future. Cost is $1,995 for the CD-ROM version.

Finding prospects and donors by ZIP code has long been a favorite way for those doing direct marketing. It can pinpoint wealth, or status, or both. Consider ZIP code 10021 on the upper east side of New York. It remains the home of 1,500 *Social Register* households, the single greatest aggregation of high-society types in the country. That ZIP code, perhaps as no surprise, has those who make the largest political donations.

For his book *Privilege, Power, and Place: The Geography of the American Upper Class*, urban geographer Stephen Richard Higley analyzed names in the 1988 *Social Register*. It annually registers the names, home addresses, family details, and club affiliations of the 25,000 families considered "high society." The summer edition of the register gives vacation addresses, plus names and gross tonnage of the yachts of those listed.

Higley found that one out of ten *Social Register* listees lived in New York, but around the country eight out of ten now live in the suburbs. Many have moved to Sunbelt states. After New York, other cities with high numbers in the book are Philadelphia, Boston, Washington, and San Francisco. It is no surprise those cities are most prominent; the book has a self-perpetuating aspect. Those in the book are added or subtracted based on recommendation by those already in the book.

Incidentally, South Dakota was the only state with no resident in the 1994 *Social Register*. Wealth alone will not gain one's entry into the book. If it did, perhaps some of those who sold property to turn the frontier home of Wild Bill Hickok and his friend Calamity Jane into the booming casino-heavy Deadwood may have qualified. (Deadwood, South Dakota, ZIP code 57732)

If you don't need to zero in to each ZIP code, use *The Sourcebook of County Demographics* from the same publisher. The CD-ROM version costs $695. Another sourcebook is available by census tract, also on CD-ROM, for $2,995. These resources include population projections through the year 2000.

Call 1-800-292-2224 (for the east coast office) to get a catalog of CACI products and a sample diskette for several counties in Connecticut, New Jersey, and New York. Or call the west coast office at 1-800-394-3690.

If you want to know what marketing surveys and reports are available for your area, *FINDEX* can give that information on magnetic tape or CD-ROM. Call Cambridge Information Group at 1-800-843-7751.

GUIDES TO GRANTS

Publishers of grant guides discovered that putting the data on a CD-ROM was a wonderfully efficient way to deliver the good news about what is available from whom. There would be no more looking in the back of the directory for the million (or so it seemed) entries under "health care" or whatever, then turning to the entry to discover some disqualifying information. Some of that back-and-forthing is still necessary, but it is much quicker and the results are better. For example, one can print out the best sounding grants right from the disc. No more fumbling with those heavy books at the copy machine.

Putting grant guides on CD-ROM was a natural progression. First, of course, there were the guides in print format, in books. Then some became available on floppy disks with the necessary disk-shuffle because the whole works would not fit on one floppy. Some were offered online through DIALOG and other online vendors. That was helpful, but the minutes and dollars ticked away very quickly with that old online anxiety setting in. Next, CD-ROM became a desirable media, for all the same reasons as other publishers had discovered this to be true.

Several grant guides on CD-ROM are available; more will be coming.

Grants Database is from Knight-Ridder Information On-Disc, with information provided from The Oryx Press. It has approximately 8,900 grants from the usual funding possibilities for $850 with bimonthly updates and a link to DIALOG online. It is searchable by subject area, sponsor, grant amount and availability, and title words. Complete contact information is given for each grant. Call KR Information at 1-800-334-2564.

Prospector's Choice is from Taft at 1-800-877-TAFT. It's listed as "The Electronic Source Profiling 8,000 corporate and foundation grant makers." There are regional versions (on 3.5-inch diskettes only) as well as a national version in both formats, CD-ROM or eight diskettes. The price ranges from $295 for a regional directory to $795 for the national version.

This CD-ROM product combines biographical information on officers and directors of corporations and foundations as well as a listing of recent grants. With its Query System, a researcher can search and retrieve information using geographical or grant-type access.

Grants on Disk! was new in 1995 from Taft. It promises a listing of 120,000 recently awarded cash grants, available on a CD-ROM as a subscription with updates for $695 a year. It gives grant recipients by name, city, and state; dollar amount of grant; purpose and type of grant; type of recipient organization; and grantor's headquarters with contact information. Call Taft at 1-800-877-TAFT.

The Chronicle Guide to Grants from the *Chronicle of Philanthropy* offers this resource either in a diskette edition on 3.5-inch high-density disks ($295) or in the CD-ROM edition ($395), both for IBM-compatible PCs. Emphasis here is on newly announced grants with listings of recent grants that a foundation has awarded. This is updated every other month, offering information on over 10,000 corporate and foundation grants. The CD-ROM edition includes thousands more. A "Quick Search" feature brings the user up to speed quickly and allows searches by state, foundation, topic, amount, recipient, or a combination of those features, making it very useful. Call 1-800-287-6072.

COMING SOON

A CD-ROM with the Foundation Center's database of foundation and corporate grantmakers is due in 1996. When available, that will provide an excellent electronic resource for nonprofit organizations. Call the Foundation Center at 1-800-424-9836 for availability and price information.

Sources of Foundations, from Orca Knowledge Systems, is available in a Windows version on CD-ROM or on disks for Windows, DOS, or Macintosh. With it, the researcher can use keywords to find a list of foundations that support that subject area. Full information is given: name, address, telephone number, and contact person for foundations; monetary range, restrictions, and application guidelines for grants; with a list of recent grants. The national version, in both formats, costs $399, with an optional add-on of foundation directors and trustees for $125.

Regional and state versions are available on disk. *Corporate Foundations and Giving,* on disk, gives somewhat the same information. It costs $239, and annual updates are $95. *Federal Domestic Assistance* is $245, with $80 updates twice a year. Realizing that many nonprofit staff members now use their computers as we used to use books, Orca has several electronic books on disk.

For additional information or to order, call Orca in San Anselmo, California, at 1-800-868-ORCA Request a demo disk so you can "try before you buy."

The official guide to 1,300 grant programs administered by 51 federal agencies is the *Catalog of Federal Domestic Assistance.* It gives full data on those programs, with program objectives and goals, types of assistance offered, eligibility requirements, examples of funded projects, and criteria for selecting proposals. Best of all, it tells how to apply for each program, with phone contacts, and tips for writing proposals.

This is on nine floppy diskettes or on a CD-ROM. Both cost the same, $60 for the current issue, or $100 for an annual subscription, including the update. Instead of juggling all the diskettes, the CD-ROM version seems much easier to use, assuming you have the necessary CD-ROM drive. (If you don't, you probably skipped this whole chapter.) This resource shows the capacity of one CD-ROM. The *Catalog* takes up only 5 percent of the CD-ROM capacity, so several other government documents from the Department of Commerce's National Economic, Social, and Environmental Database—including books, magazines, reports, and tables—are included on the disc.

As funding from the federal government is becoming either more scarce, or harder to pinpoint, this source is very useful, for a bargain price. Call 1-202-708-5126 for more information or to order.

The online equivalent is the *Federal Assistance Programs Retrieval System (FAPRS)*. It gives access to the *Catalog*. Call that same number for information on *FAPRS*. It is available for a $50 annual fee.

In 1995 a Windows version of the *Catalog* was introduced. Called *Federal Money Retriever*, it makes looking for a federal grant almost as much fun as playing a computer game with a pot of funding gold as the prize. It uses those familiar Windows point-and-click commands to search for appropriate grants from all agencies simultaneously. The search can then be refined by keyword and printed out. There is no more flipping back and forth from the index to the grant details, it's all a smooth search.

Federal Money Retriever is $195 from IDI Valley Technologies at 1-800-804-5270 or 1-208-734-5663.

Here is an idea to investigate for any of these Gale CD-ROMs. If you are in an institution, a college or university, for example, and the main library and other libraries around campus have Gale directories networked through their own online computer system, you could subscribe to the IBM network version for a few hundred dollars more and have it in your own office through a local area network (LAN), probably already operating on campus. As mentioned before, networking is worth investigating for access to the business databases also. Networking of resources around campus is now fairly easy as many vendors offer special networking pricing for their products. This is less expensive than stand-alone access and may put some of these services on your office computers.

Another, the *Federal Grants and Funding Locator on CD-ROM* gives 35 fields of data per record on 1,300 grant programs, updated and published twice per year.

On CD-ROM, using the DOS system, it is $295 from Staff Directories, Ltd. Call 1-703-739-2964 to order or, for information, call 1-703-739-0900.

BIOGRAPHICAL DIRECTORIES AND INDEXES

Here's the classic, perhaps the most useful guide for prospect research in most nonprofit organizations. *Biography and Genealogy Master Index CD-ROM* from Gale Research, Inc. The numbers are a bit staggering: Source citations of 2,100 volumes of 700 current and retrospective biographical directories on more than 4 million people. All on two discs.

Note, this is a guide *to* the information. It does not, like many directories, give the needed information. It tells you where to find it. As a first step to biographical research, it can't be beat. Instead of randomly searching through publications that may or may not have what you need, this hits the target. Type in the name and you get the hits in a second, assuming the name is there.

This guide covers people from the beginning of time to today's news makers. Many times, you will need to qualify the name further, or narrow the possibilities by using a name plus a known fact (birth year, or geographical location) to get citations to the right person, not a lot of others with the same name.

Each citation provides the biographee's name, birth and death years (if available), and the full source publication information. A nice feature is that it can be customized to highlight publications available in the library where this CD-ROM is used. You can print out your information or copy it to your own floppy disk for use later.

The master index on CD-ROM is $1,250 per year with subsequent updates for $375, bringing it up to date with current volumes of indexed reference sources. Call 1-800-877-GALE.

Many nonprofit offices prefer the microfiche card version, called **Bio-Base**, available in an updated 1995 edition. It requires only an inexpensive microfiche reader (preferably with a printer attached, but not essential). For approximately $1,000 it gives access to millions of names, in hundreds of directories. Many offices begin their biographical research with this tool, then call their public library for information from the source cited. It's from Gale at the above number.

Because many public and college libraries have this important tool, either in CD-ROM, on microfiche, or in print format, you might want to pack up your list of names and use this master index to see how it works for your major donor list before purchasing it for your office.

For those who have waited for it, *Who's Who in America* may be out on a CD-ROM when you read this. It is expected by mid-1996. It will be called **Marquis Who's Who Plus** and one disc will include the four United States regional sets and the seven professional directories now published as separate volumes. Wow! Won't that be wonderful? It promises 490,000 living notables—and 6,000 who have passed away since 1985. The cost is expected to be between $1,500 - $2,000 annually, with quarterly updates included at that price.

As a former librarian who spent most of my life, (it seems), looking for biographical information in one or more *Who's Who*, it will be heaven to have easy access to all the volumes to- gether. There is currently a print index to all *Who's Who* volumes, but a CD-ROM with all the volumes together seems ideal.

DONOR AND FAMILY INFORMATION

Town and Country magazine profiles wealthy socialites in each issue. Waltman Associates has indexed all issues between 1986 and 1995. It is available on a CD-ROM that includes over 60,000 names with the person's occupation and reference to the magazine issue and page. Each December, the magazine lists donors who gave $1 million or more. The CD-ROM costs $149.

CD-ROMs: Consider These for the Nonprofit Office

National Donors, on CD-ROM, lists more than 100,000 donors and their individual gifts to nonprofit organizations. It can be accessed by name, giving category, recipient, and amount. From Waltman Associates, it will be available in mid-1996 for $499. Call 1-612-388-0772.

4

CD-ROMs: Try Them Out at a Library

> *"I had always imagined paradise as a kind of library."*
>
> Jorge Luis Borges

Even though you can get almost all of your information needs from printed directories or online services, you should check out what new electronic resources are available at public or academic libraries. What is available will depend on the size of the library and whether it has had adequate funding during recent years. The most exciting new technological products in many libraries during the last ten years are CD-ROMs.

CD-ROMs are for library users, often called "end users," to use without librarian help. Unlike online searching, the meter does not keep clicking. The price was paid up front by the library. Although there may be fees for printing information, in some cases, the only thing that will make you hurry in your research is if there are others waiting to use the terminals.

BIOGRAPHICAL RESOURCES

Refer to the previous chapter for biographical resources often found in public and academic libraries. The most valuable is the *Biography and Genealogy Master Index* from Gale. On microfiche, it has been an important reference tool in many development offices. Now available on CD-ROM, it is even more useful.

Long a classic in its print version, *Current Biography* on CD-ROM pulls together over fifty years of profiling political leaders, celebrities, top educators, authors, sports stars, and wealthy persons. It is more than a directory, as it gives many details about the person, sometimes even salary or annual income, and net-worth details. It tells interests, sometimes favorite charities, and family information. The CD-ROM costs $188 from H.W. Wilson at 1-800-367-6770.

As mentioned in the last chapter, *Who's Who in America*, with regional and professional biographical directories from Reed Publishing, should be available on CD-ROM by the time you read this. If so, it will be in many libraries. Ask for it there.

PERIODICAL AND NEWSPAPER INDEXES AND ABSTRACTS

Although computerization has changed all types of research, perhaps in no way has the general public benefited more than by the introduction of electronic indexing of magazine and newspaper articles.

In the nonprofit office, there are many reasons to use each. Say, for example, you are doing prospect or donor research. While getting information from directories is useful, there is not much human interest in those just-the-facts books. The story of the person beyond the position is what you need. It often can be found in magazines and newspapers. Keep in mind that the best ones about your donors will probably be those that cover your city, state, or region, unless the person is known nationally. Then, national newspapers and magazines may have featured the person in a lengthy article.

Either way, you will want to find tidbits of information that may link the prospect to your organization. What are the person's interests? What is the source of income? What charities has the person been involved with?

Clues to the person's net worth is always helpful. Using periodical indexes, it is possible to tap into professional journals that may give salary or profit data. For example, the *American Lawyer* gives an annual "profits-per-partner" list for top firms in selected large cities. Other professional journals have similar information, giving basic income figures for that field.

Looking for those living in high-wealth ZIP codes? *American Demographics Magazine* occasionally has articles telling which ZIP codes have the most affluent residents. Periodical indexes are a good way to look for leading African American business executives and entrepreneurs.

Development officers looking for information on corporate donors will also want to check those periodical and newspaper indexes before contacting the company officials for help. Check those indexes for ideas about fund-raising

campaigns and planning special events. Or brush up on management techniques by reading about the recent theories.

Those old enough remember the green *Readers' Guide to Periodical Literature* indexes used in high schools. The user had to flip through several volumes to get needed citations. Then, in the late 1970s, Information Access Company introduced a popular public library resource called *Magazine Index*. With a microfilm index preloaded into a microfilm reader, a user could get several years of citations at one glance. It offered only a straight alphabetical subject listing, but was a big improvement over print volumes.

In the 1980s, as technology evolved, that index became a CD-ROM-based product that allowed more sophisticated search strategies. The index covered more years and came in a "package deal" with computer, CD-ROM drive, and printer. It gave easy access to periodical literature and was used in hundreds of libraries around the country.

Competition for this type of indexing became very competitive as other companies began providing products to libraries needing, more or less, the same thing. From the initial straight subject indexing, companies produced variations of the same, with increased abstracting, then full-text access. The products were available in different versions, for large or small public libraries, or in an academic version for scholastic journals, and by specific subject, such as computers, business, and health.

Currently, ***InfoTrac*** is available in several versions on CD-ROM. (And, online through Knight-Ridder DIALOG and Knowledge Index, through CompuServe.) Small public libraries may have ***Magazine Index Plus***, which covers 400 magazines plus current issues of the *New York Times* and the *Wall Street Journal*. ***Magazine Index Select*** is a smaller version, indexing 200 periodicals. ***Magazine ASAP Plus*** provides full text for over 100 of the most popular general-interest magazines indexed in *Magazine Index Plus*.

Larger versions from Information Access are the ***General Periodicals Index*** for public libraries, with indexing to 1,100 periodicals plus three major newspapers, the *New York Times*, the *Christian Science Monitor,* and the *Wall Street Journal.* An *Academic Index* does 400 journals, and an *Expanded Academic Index* indexes 1,500 journals. From those, *Expanded Academic Index ASAP*, gives full text to 400 of those magazines.

InfoTrac's competition for periodical indexing for the library market is a selection of databases and information delivery systems from UMI, University Microfilms, Inc. That company is known for putting publications on microfilm for archival purposes. UMI came out with their *ProQuest* series. Each version falls into one of the following categories: abstract and index, full text, and full image.

That last category gives abstracts and indexing with material in full-image format. Unlike many databases, in readable, but boring looking ASCII format, this shows each page as it originally appeared in the publication. The articles were digitally scanned into the database, capturing all the charts, graphics, and photos that were part of the magazine's communication technique.

UMI's *Periodical Abstracts Research I* indexes and abstracts 1,000 titles from general-reference journals. *Research II* does the same for 1,600 journals plus articles from the last six months of the *Wall Street Journal* and the *New York Times*. *Periodical Abstracts*, *Select*, and *Periodical Abstracts Library* are versions for smaller public libraries.

Other versions from UMI, called *ProQuest PQ*, combine newspaper and periodical coverage, some in a "package" plan with microfilm archives of the covered material.

For those doing business research, as most nonprofit organizations must sometimes do, UMI's *Business Dateline* gives full-text access to articles from 450 regional business publications. It's great for checking out those companies that you are considering as potential corporate donors. The full-image CD-ROM products follow a similar progression from a small number of periodicals covered to more extensive coverage. They are called *General Periodicals Research I and II* and also *Select* and *Library*. Full-image articles can be printed from the workstation.

Because UMI has long been in the business of providing journals and newspapers on microfilm to libraries, it has a very effective on-demand document delivery system through the UMI InfoStore. Once you know the citation, you can order by phone by calling 1-800-248-0360 or 1-415-433-5500. You may also mail or fax your order to UMI, or use one of the on-line services accessing periodicals in the UMI database, putting the charge on a credit card.

H.W. Wilson, the company that started it all with those green guides, has a CD-ROM product called, like those print versions, *Readers' Guide to Periodical Literature*. It indexes 230 general-interest magazines and the *New York Times*. *Readers' Guide Abstracts* adds summaries for 60,000 articles since 1985. One distinct characteristic of this index, although it is updated monthly, is that it connects to the online version, called *Wilsonline* and *FirstSearch (OCLC)*, updated twice a week.

Another library vendor, EBSCO, checked in with *Magazine Article Summaries* and *Academic Abstracts*.

Got that straight? It's all a bit complex, as each company tries to outdo the next with coverage and backfiles. The most important thing to remember and realize is that wonderful magazine indexes are now available at most libraries. Find out what is there, then use it for your research needs. If you have not done this type of research in the past few years, you'll be pleased with the technological progress. Most libraries have indexes from one or the other of these companies, each service giving adequate coverage.

A new and very important feature is finding these indexed on a library's OPAC, online catalog. Some can be accessed from home or the office with your dial-up modem. Many of the same products on CD-ROM are now available through OCLC as part of *FirstSearch*. Ask your local librarian for assistance.

NEWSPAPER INDEXES ON CD-ROM

No publications capture the life of a community and its citizens as well as the local newspaper. Most public libraries have backfiles of the local papers on microfilm, but until recently the indexing was not as complete as is now possible with electronics. Subject indexing may get you to the main topic of the article, but cannot pick up every name in the article. That's the wonderful feature possible with electronic full-text newspapers, accessible online or on CD-ROM, where each word or name can be found.

National Newspaper Index, a CD-ROM from Information Access, indexes the last four years of the *New York Times*, the *Wall Street Journal*, the *Christian Science Monitor*, the *Los Angeles Times*, and the *Washington Post*. It's updated monthly and is available online with DIALOG and through Knowledge Index on CompuServe. Note, this is not full text, indexing each word. To get that, you need a CD-ROM version of the complete newspaper. (See the list of those elsewhere [p. 62] in this book.)

Newspaper Abstracts and *Newspaper Abstracts National*, both from UMI on CD-ROMs, provide abstract coverage of leading newspapers.

NewsBank, from NewsBank, Inc., indexes articles from about 500 regional newspapers, back to 1981. With many newspapers on *CD News* in full text, it includes both national newspapers, plus local and regional ones. Public and other libraries often have this resource available for students working on subject term papers, but it is, of course, useful for all research.

MULTICULTURAL ELECTRONIC RESOURCES

Ethnic NewsWatch, on CD-ROM from SoftLine Information, indexes and gives full text of more than 25,000 articles from over 100 newspapers and magazines from the ethnic and minority press in the United States, beginning in 1991. This is a wonderful way to find news and trends among ethnic groups and names and information on their leaders. Publications are from Jewish, East European, African American, Native American, Asian, Middle Eastern, and Hispanic sources. It includes bibliography information for publications covered. It can be searched in Spanish as well as English and is online with *NEXIS-LEXIS*.

A diskette product called *Afro-American Insight* (from Afro-Link Software) lists African American businesses, black mayors and elected officials, black colleges, and other topics of special interest to African Americans.

Chicano Database on CD-ROM, from the Chicano Studies Library at the University of California, Berkeley, gives bibliographic citations on the Mexican-American experience. It includes indexing of Chicano periodicals back to 1967 and has more recently expanded to include other Spanish-speaking groups in this country.

For historic research, *The American Indian: A Multimedia Encyclopedia* offers a Who Was Who from many American tribes as well as document reproductions from the National Archives.

Though not electronic, there are many good reference tools available on African Americans, Hispanic Americans, and Asian Americans. Included are who's who type volumes from Gale Research. Ask for help at the library.

Although all of these are very useful resources for current events research, the most useful probably is the CD-ROM version of your own local big-city newspaper, or a regional newspaper, if you are in a small community. More than likely a reference librarian will be able to tell you if such a product is available. Using your own CD-ROM equipment, a subscription to the local newspaper on CD-ROM may cost $2,000 to $3,000 annually. My recommendation is to use it at the library, if possible, then use your online access for quick searches between library visits.

Using historical newspapers can be an important resource for family donor research, or even institutional research. Until recently, finding microfilm editions of old newspapers, with adequate indexing to make them useful, has been a hit-or-miss affair. Luckily, the Library of Congress and the National Endowment for the Humanities are directing a massive campaign to preserve newspapers throughout the country. The United States Newspaper Program (USNP) seeks to locate scattered runs of local newspapers and consolidate them into complete files before microfilming the collection. Each state is working to document the newspapers published in that state from the eighteenth century to the present.

ONLINE LIBRARY CATALOGS

In those days before computers appeared everywhere, in the dark ages of the 1970s, many librarians determined it was time to close the time-honored card catalog and store the data electronically to be accessed on a computer terminal. These online public access catalogs, called OPACs, are now the norm. Although some librarians (myself included) lamented the demise of those old card catalogs, there is no doubt that the OPACs have many advantages—with some disadvantages.

OPACs are more than just card catalogs. They can tell library patrons what is on order, what books are "on the shelf," which are checked out, and when the item is due back. Circulation procedures were streamlined with OPACs, and keeping track of who had materials checked out became easier. Some libraries mount additional databases onto the OPACs, including periodical indexes or community bulletin boards. Vendors of library indexes offered database licensing agreements so their products could be used, for example, on college campuses at all college libraries. Some public libraries are able to do the same at their branches.

For research purposes, what mattered is that accessibility to the collections was much improved. Instead of offering the capacity to search only by author, title, or subject, this opened new possibilities, including keyword and Boolean searching. Keyword searching means the computer will search for every occurrence of a particular word. Boolean searching allows the researcher to use AND, NOT, or OR to narrow or broaden searches. It is possible to limit the search by date of publication, by publisher, or by other factors.

That's fine if you are in the library and can use the OPAC there. If not, best of all, with OPACs many libraries permit remote access to their online catalog via a telephone line using a modem. Within the next few years, more libraries will offer this service. Also, there is the Internet. Several university libraries and a few public libraries can be accessed that way from remote corners of the country—and world. (More on that in Chapter 13.)

Examples of online access to a host of library databases are the *OCLC EPIC* and *FirstSearch* systems. *EPIC* offers access at the library, with librarian assistance. *FirstSearch* lets the end user do the search—either in the library or online. The value of OPAC access to multiple libraries is if you are looking for a specific book, especially one not found in your locality. Or it can be for information about an author who you think has written something, published, but who knows where. With the OCLC database holding over 27 million records, there is a good chance you will find what you need.

Throughout the country, thousands of libraries are connected to *OCLC (Online Computer Library Center)*. Most began using its online services for cataloging their own collections, using the extensive *OCLC Online Union Catalog*. Services expanded as libraries connected to OCLC could access periodical and newspaper indexes, full-text journal articles, and business directories.

Your local library's contract with OCLC will determine if they offer *OCLC FirstSearch* or *EPIC* services. Although now the services may be available mostly through academic libraries, for use by students and faculty members, they are spreading to public libraries. With these OCLC services you can access periodical indexes. Ask about these services at the library you use.

Documents, be they articles or reports, can be ordered from OCLC for fax delivery within an hour ("rush fax") or for delivery by the end of the next business day.

Instead of the OCLC system, some libraries are affiliated with the *Colorado Alliance of Research Libraries (CARL)* offering access to about 500 public and academic library catalogs. CARL can be accessed through your modem by dialing 1-303-758-1551, or look for it on the Internet. Once in the system, you can browse in individual library online catalogs (OPACs), using the same search procedures. Other commercially available databases can be searched with a password, available for a fee. Or, in some communities, the password may be your library card number, which will gain access to periodical, journal, and newspaper indexes.

CARL Uncover is an online index to tables of content for thousands of magazines and journals, covering about 6 million articles. The service is very up to date and the actual articles, once identified, can be ordered and delivered to your fax machine within 24 hours. *CARL* will fax an article for about $10.

ELECTRONIC BUSINESS, CORPORATE DIRECTORIES AND INDEXES

In the previous chapter's overview on CD-ROM products, many are listed that are fairly expensive. Many were developed for use either in the securities business or corporate libraries, and then picked up as super library resources. Because of this, a library may be the best place to use some of the comprehensive CD-ROM products giving corporate information that you may not be able to afford to have in your own office. (Please refer to Chapter 3 for information on CD-ROM business directories.)

Many of these products are also online, but, because you can use CD-ROMs at a library without those pesky online charges, you can get a feel for what information you can get from each product and how to access it. After some experience searching on a CD-ROM, you will be better able to determine if you want to purchase the product on CD-ROM or get the information online.

Good examples of business directories at libraries on CD-ROM are the *Disclosure* products. *Compact Disclosure U.S.*

gives financial data on about 11,000 companies. *Compact Disclosure/World* does the same for those hard-to-find international companies.

As you may have guessed, the same database companies doing general periodicals and newspaper CD-ROMs have products that concentrate on business publications, with indexes, abstracts, or full-text access.

Business Index, from Information Access, is part of the *InfoTrac* system. It covers 300 business journals, over 50 regional business publications, and business subjects from general magazines, plus the *Wall Street Journal* and the *New York Times*. It gives subject and author indexing, plus some keyword access. *Business ASAP*, another CD-ROM product, carries the full text of articles indexed in the *Business Index*.

From UMI, it's *ABI/INFORM* for business periodicals. It gives abstracts of articles, for about 800 publications.

Another index with abstracts is *Wilson Business Abstracts* on CD-ROM, from H.W. Wilson. Abstracts and indexing cover 350 business magazines and business issues from the *Wall Street Journal* and the *New York Times*. Online, this service is on *Wilsonline* and from OCLC's *FirstSearch*.

Business NewsBank is useful because it reproduces business articles with full text from 450 daily newspapers (probably including ones in your region) and 150 weeklies. These come on CD-ROMs, updated monthly. Because it includes local and regional newspapers, it is more apt to include those small and privately held companies than would the national press, although those are also included. Verbatim news releases from companies across the nation are included. This is part of a family of CD-ROM products from NewsBank, all including full-text articles from newspapers and periodicals, designed for the library market.

Nonprofit organizations often need census data as new service sites are considered. The U.S. Census Bureau now makes available most of its population, economic, business, and housing data on a CD-ROM available in many libraries. City and county population and economic figures are offered from CACI's *Sourcebooks on CD-ROM*.

PROFESSIONAL DIRECTORIES ON CD-ROM

Directory of Physicians in the United States. The classic print directory listing over 633,000 physicians licensed to practice medicine in the United States is now on a CD-ROM from the American Medical Association. Call 1-312-645-5000.

Lawyers are listed with some biographical information and firm affiliation in the *Martindale-Hubbell Law Directory on CD-ROM*. It's from Reed Publishing at $995, including quarterly updates.

Reed does the similar *Official ABMS Directory of Medical Specialists Plus* that includes over 50,000 physicians. It is $1,195, including updates. Call Reed Publishing at 1-800-323-3288 or 1-908-771-8711.

AUTHORS

CONTEMPORARY AUTHORS ON CD. For more than 30 years, Gale Research, Inc., has compiled data on authors. They have covered over 100,000 authors, novelists, poets, playwrights, journalists, and nonfiction writers. Now, instead of trying to find the one you need in over 100 print volumes, use this one CD-ROM, available at many libraries.

Because this picks up some not-well-known authors, it is useful. Best of all, it tells how to contact the writer, with agent information included. It gives a summary of the writer's career, with a listing of writings, plus sidelights. These, including interviews and sometimes short autobiographical sketches, give personal insights into interests and social concerns.

It's around $3,650, a good candidate to use at a library, if you can find it there. (If not, use the print volumes.)

WILSON AUTHOR BIOGRAPHIES on CD-ROM is from a classic set of print reference books used in most libraries, covering authors from the classical era to the present. It costs $299 on disc from H.W. Wilson at 1-800-367-6770.

When searching for information on an author, it is nice to know what that person has written. H.W. Wilson's *Cumulative Book Index (CBI)* lists over 565,000 books published since 1982 in English worldwide on a CD-ROM, or online from Wilson. While you are connected online, you can access the *Wilson Name Authority File*. That gives preferred forms for over 650,000 personal, corporate, and publication names and titles.

LIBRARY REGULATIONS

Public libraries, of course, are open for all, but you may be prohibited from checking out materials if you are not in the jurisdiction funding the library. Many large cities, with surrounding suburban communities, now have reciprocal borrowing privileges. Except for those mysteries you need for late-night reading, most of what you will need for your nonprofit research will be reference resources used in the libraries. In public libraries, anyone can use them, but there will, in many instances, be restrictions on any online searching done by the librarian to answer your requests.

Sometimes the library will offer extensive reference help for a cost-per-search fee. For example, the San Francisco Public Library launched a program offering in-depth reference service in 1995. Under the program, librarians will research a topic, locate the documents, and send the information to the client within approximately 24 hours for a charge of $60 per hour. If an online charge is needed, there are additional charges. If this fee service is appealing, see if such is available at your local library.

Should you need general, but not reference, books in your research, books not found in your public library may be requested via interlibrary loan. As more libraries have their catalogs available on an electronic database network of regional or state holdings, this is becoming easier. If not there, then the librarian may have access to the national OCLC database to determine who owns what you need.

Where the Information Is

If the public library does not have what you need, a local college or university library may have the necessary resources. Many community- or state-funded institutions are open to residents for research only; no borrowing privileges. Regulations vary. In California, for example, there is a charge of $50 to use state academic libraries, after showing that state's driver's license as identification.

If the nearby college or university is private, there will probably be restrictions. Often arrangements can be made, upon application, to use the facilities. Sometimes you can pay a fee for limited library privileges. It may be steep: like $275 to use Harvard's college libraries for three months. Library cards elsewhere range from $50 on up. One possibility for a discounted fee, is as a member of a Friends of the Library group, or if you are a graduate of the school. Interlibrary loan privileges are usually restricted to those directly affiliated with the academic institution.

Perhaps the most important reason you should use libraries for some of your research is that you can save money by doing some of your research there. Despite the appeal of doing your own online searching, that glitz comes with a price tag. With careful analysis of what electronic resources are available at the library, and planning ahead, you can get a lot of information on your individual and corporate donors there. For free!

5

DIALOG: Online
to the World

*"I have an anthropologist's point of view about
technology... Technology is a tool and every
culture is going to both shape a tool and be
shaped by a tool."*

Laura Breeden, *infoActive*, July/August 1994

Anyone doing research in a nonprofit office must consider online searching. It is not a new technology, but it is a constantly changing technology, now easier to access and, often, less expensive than in years past.

For some researchers in nonprofit offices, information on online searching and DIALOG is old stuff. An American Prospect Research Association, as it was then known, survey in 1994 showed 70.5 percent of its members were using electronic databases, and DIALOG was the preferred in-house service used by 44.3 percent of those using electronic databases or CD-ROMs.

Many researchers noted in the survey that they had been doing online searching for years. As recently as five years ago, however, DIALOG or other online searching was done mostly by researchers in fairly large organizations or by smaller organizations who were fortunate to have a researcher with previous online experience, such as a trained reference librarian or information broker.

In 1991, a study, done by the Institute for Nonprofit Organization Management in San Francisco, analyzed the use of computers and online information systems by nonprofit organizations. Of the 206 organizations surveyed, 66 percent used computers, but only 17 percent were using them for some type of online service. At that time, most responding to the survey knew about online possibilities but couldn't crank up either the need or the nerve to actually do it.

Gradually things are changing. If the survey were done in 1995, my guess is that almost 100 percent would be using computers, and many more than 17 percent would use them for research. One reason is that online searching is just plain easier than it used to be. This is partly because most new computers come loaded with communication software and a modem. That's all the equipment needed, plus an account with DIALOG, to get started. Later, this book will tell about database access through commercial online services.

DIALOG remains the granddaddy of all online database vendors. As the survey showed, it is the vendor most often used for research by nonprofit organizations.

The reason is simple. The DIALOG information collection contains millions of documents drawn from sources throughout the world. Its databases contain company and market intelligence, full-text newspapers and wire services, company directories and biographical resources. As such, the information available through your office computer, equipped with a modem, is overwhelming. It may also be a bit scary. Information in online format can be expensive. The meter ticks away by the second, and, as it ticks, an inexperienced searcher may begin to panic, trying to find the needle in the haystack of information.

In 1988 DIALOG was purchased by Knight-Ridder, but the name did not change until January 1995. The company is now Knight-Ridder Information. It has two online services, one the familiar DIALOG and the other DataStar, providing information on Europe. CD-ROM products used to be *DIALOG On-Disc*; they are now *KR Information OnDisc*. In most cases,

Knight-Ridder Information DIALOG will be called DIALOG throughout this book.

As the information era is changing access to all types of information, so DIALOG is changing itself to keep up with the new ways people are looking for data. From its early days, with huge mainframe computers in Palo Alto holding the databases that subscribers hooked into, to today when users want more user-friendly access, DIALOG keeps inventing more ways to access those databases. It must meet, or keep one step ahead of, the competition.

In order to be both cost effective for the professional searchers, and user friendly for the novice or occasional searchers, DIALOG continues to make changes. Such a change led to the adoption of a Windows-based communication package when that software became a standard system for many desktop personal computers. With that, users no longer needed to remember cumbersome commands, the new system featured familiar point-and-click techniques.

For example, *KR BusinessBase*, from KR DIALOG provides easy access for business searchers. Users can click on icons and folders, leading to various databases, for speedier, more thorough searches. This allows users to type a ticker symbol or an approximation of a company name, then point and click on icons to find the needed answers from a wide range of DIALOG databases. Other Windows-based products are planned.

A joint venture with Advanced Research Technologies, Inc., (ART) will use Windows interfaces to databases for novice end users. Each custom program will be designed for specific groups of searchers.

The cost of data now varies greatly as there are more ways to find the same information. *Forbes*, April 11, 1994, stated that access to airline schedules costs $48 an hour on DIALOG, but only $2 an hour on the consumer-oriented America Online! This book will tell how to find less expensive ways to access certain databases.

Another reason for the increase of online searching by those in nonprofit organizations is the emphasis put on this type of research at local, regional, and national meetings of the Association of Professional Researchers for Advancement (APRA) and the National Society of Fund Raising Executives (NSFRE) and at Council for Advancement and Support of Education (CASE) conferences. This exposure to the possibilities and the methods for both novice and experienced researchers at meetings has encouraged many to do online research.

Still, there are others who would benefit from online research who are not yet doing it. Perhaps this book will give the gentle shove that is needed. Read on to discover what is available.

The plan of this book is to cut out unnecessary information about research in general and zero in on what is most useful for the nonprofit researcher. Honestly, you will never need most of the databases available, unless you want to research coffee production in Ethiopia (on *COFFEELINE*), molecular formulae (on *CHEMNAME*), or vessels loading cargo (on *PIERS* Imports). (The object seems to be to find a name for the database that fits the data.) DIALOG's databases actually go from A to Z: from *ABI/INFORM* to *Zoological Record Online*.

Now there are several ways to access DIALOG databases. (They will be explained later.) Previously the only way to get them was with your own DIALOG account and password. It's still a very good way because of DIALOG customer support, training, and documentation. A toll-free customer hotline gives assistance with any problem concerning logon or search procedures.

New users can participate in full-day or half-day introductory seminars in many regions. Where available, lunch-hour sessions are available for specific groups. Some regional DIALOG offices give prospect research seminars, especially for nonprofit offices. Also, APRA conferences and regional meetings often have computer labs available with time to experiment with that service. Next time you attend such a meeting, bring along some hard research questions and give DIALOG a try.

With a personal computer, a modem, communication software, and a telephone line, you can connect to DIALOG. Because of arrangements with local telecommunications companies, DIALOG is just a local call away, in most areas, but you pay for each minute connected to DIALOG. Cost varies by database and goes from a low of less than a $1 per minute way up into the ionosphere. For example, one database is $5.75 per minute, equalling $345 per hour. Talk about online anxiety. Luckily, you probably don't care about European agrochemical products.

The best way to begin with DIALOG is to contact Knight-Ridder Information sales at 1-800-334-2564 (or 1-800-3-DIA-LOG) for information on opening an account. They will send a standard service agreement to be completed and returned with a check or your organization's purchase order for $295. This brings all that is needed to begin using DIALOG, plus credit for $100 free online connect time, to be used within the first 90 days. It cannot be used for type, display, or print charges. (Those with an Internet connection can contact DIALOG at http://www.dialog.com.)

DIALOG will send an invoice each month for your charges. Each year, a service fee of $75 keeps your password active. DIALOG offers many special pricing options, including a flat rate, based on past usage. Sometimes there are discount rates for new members. Ask when you sign up. Even if you are not normally a DIALOG user, it might be worth exploring such an offer before a major capital campaign or major donor search.

First, it's important to know what's on it for you. With nonprofit research, the most typical searches deal with people, companies, demographics, foundations, and other funding sources. With access to a variety of databases, such as those available with DIALOG access, you could conceivably sit at your computer and find most of what you need for donor identification and research.

There need be no expensive volumes of *Who's Who in America* on your shelves. Get information on just the names you need from the computer with the *MARQUIS WHO'S WHO* database. No more tediously clipping files from your local or regional newspapers. Just check the PAPERS file for full text access to what you need. Most large city newspapers are now available, and more regional newspapers are being added each year.

Do you want information on that company in your city? Who owns it? Who are the directors? What are the salaries of top officers? What are the annual sales? How can you get a list of companies in the state with sales over $1 million?

It's all there, online through DIALOG. For a price, of course, but the print business directories are very expensive and so are targeted mailing lists. With online, you pay only for the information you need — not all that you will never need or use.

To make searching easier, and to avoid missing just exactly the database with the information you need, DIALOG suggests you begin your search strategy with DIALINDEX. As it sounds, it searches, at one time, ALL databases or just databases in specific categories. It can be qualified: ALLBUSINESS, ALLGENERAL, ALLGOVERNMENT, ALLHUMANITIES, ALLLAW, ALLNEWS, ALLREFERENCE, ALLSCIENCE, ALLSOCIAL, ALLTEXT.

This technique is most useful for determining which file or files will be most productive for a search statement and for helping to determine how broadly or narrowly to define a search strategy. Predefined subject categories may be used, or individual databases may be specified by number.

Databases with information on your subject are identified with *DIALINDEX*, file 411. This free index gets you started and identifies where to find what you need. The most useful databases can then be ranked by number, then searched with OneSearch. OneSearch provides access to databases containing similar information, by subject, region, or format. A Duplicate Detection system feature is useful to prevent paying for the same information available from several databases.

If you are looking for authors of journal articles, use *JOURNAL NAME FINDER*, file 414. Or use file 416, *COMPANY*

NAME FINDER or file 413, *PRODUCT NAME FINDER.* All are for quick identification, with only connect-time charges.

Because computerized databases search each word in selected fields, or are full text, it is possible to pick up minute details or a combination of details hidden deeply within the data. By putting in AND commands or NOT commands, it is possible to zero in and pick out connections between two people, or connections to a person and a company, or to identify specific persons but not others with similar or the same names.

Many DIALOG databases are available through membership in CompuServe at a reduced rate after business hours. See Chapter 8 for details. If you have Internet access, you can get the Bluesheets (describing each database with search strategies) there for free.

DIALOG offers an Alert service, meaning you automatically will get new information on a person, subject, or company as it is published. For example, if a news article appears, that information will be sent to you. Or, through DIALSEARCH, someone at DIALOG will do the actual search for a small fee, using your password. For a complicated or expensive search, this may save money. It is sure to save online anxiety for new researchers. DIALOG's researchers spend all day doing similar searches and are very skilled.

Just in case you're feeling insecure as a novice searcher, and most people do feel that way, DIALOG has a way to help you. A series of *ONTAP* databases are really practice tools, designed to let you get a feel for the terrain. They work just like the big databases but are limited to a small portion of what is on the whole. All charge just 25 cents per minute ($15 per hour), with no charge for online type (or downloading). Offline prints (sent by mail to your address for a charge) are not available. Here are some sample ONTAP files similar to ones you will probably use in your research.

ONTAP ABI/INFORM. It contains selected records from 1987-1990 providing references and abstracts on management and administration.

ONTAP BOSTON GLOBE. It includes only three months in 1990, but if you live in Boston and plan to use this database, this is a good place to practice. Researchers outside of Boston can use this practice to good advantage if you plan to do newspaper research in your own and other cities as techniques are the same.

ONTAP D&B—Dun's Market Identifiers. There are 15,000 records from the 1991 version of this database available for practice.

ONTAP DIALINDEX. This groups all the ONTAP files and allows training to identify which files have the information you need. When searching in "real time," DIALINDEX is a good way to begin your searches.

As mentioned, many Knight-Ridder Information DIALOG databases are available in different formats. Organizations doing extensive research have found it financially beneficial to have their most-used databases on CD-ROM, to be used over and over again with no additional charges. Getting your local newspaper on CD-ROM may be a good idea, if it is available from Knight-Ridder Information or elsewhere.

In 1995, these newspapers are available on CD-ROM from Knight-Ridder Information. Quarterly updating is usual. Keep in mind, DIALOG is not the only source of newspapers on CD-ROM or online.

> *Boston Globe*, 1986 to present
> *Detroit Free Press*, 1988 to present
> *Los Angeles Times*, 1986 to present
> *Miami Herald*, 1988 to present
> *Newsday* and *New York Newsday*, 1988 to present (*New York Newsday* ceased publication July 16, 1995; *Newsday* continues)
> *The Philadelphia Inquirer*, 1987 to present
> *San Francisco Chronicle*, 1987 to present
> *San Jose Mercury News*, 1986 to present

Because newspaper research is so crucial for all nonprofit organizations, here is a list of what is available in the PAPERS online file in DIALOG. Data is added daily, as provided from the individual newspaper publishers.

(Akron) *Beacon Journal*, 1/88 to present
(Albany) *Times Union*, 3/86 to present
(Allentown) *Morning Call*, 1/90 to present
Anchorage Daily News, 1/89 to present
Atlantic Journal/Atlantic Constitution, 1/89 to present
(Baltimore) *Sun*, 9/90 to present
Boston Globe, 1/80 to present
Buffalo News, 1/90 to present
Charlotte Observer, 1/88 to present
Chicago Tribune, 1/85 to present
Christian Science Monitor, 1/89 to present
Cincinnati Post/Kentucky Post, 4/90 to present
(Cleveland) *Plain Dealer*, 8/91 to present
(Columbia) *State*, 1/87 to present
Columbus Dispatch, 1/88 to present
Dayton Daily News, 10/90 to present
(Denver) *Rocky Mountain News*, 6/89 to present
Detroit Free Press, 1/88 to present
(Fort Lauderdale) *Sun Sentinel*, 1/88 to present
Fresno Bee, 1/90 to present
Houston Post, 1/88 to present
Lexington Herald-Leader, 1/83 to present
(Los Angeles) *Daily News*, 1/89 to present
Los Angeles Times, 1/85 to present
(Madison) *Capital Times/Wisconsin State Journal*,
    1/90 to present
(Memphis) *The Commercial Appeal*, 6/90 to present
Miami Herald, 1/83 to present
(Minneapolis) *Star Tribune*, 1/89 to present
(New Jersey) *The Record*, 1/89 to present
(New Orleans) *The Times Picayune*, 1/89 to present
(Newport News) *Daily Press*, 4/89 to present

Newsday and *New York Newsday*, 1/87 to present (*New York Newsday* ceased publication July 16, 1995; *Newsday* continues)

(Norfolk) *The Virginian-Pilot/The Ledger Star*, 1/90 to present

Orlando Sentinel, 1/88 to present

Palm Beach Post, 1/89 to present

Philadelphia Daily News, 1/83 to present

Philadelphia Inquirer, 1/83 to present

(Phoenix) *Arizona Republic/ Phoenix Gazette*, 1/86 to present

Pittsburgh Post-Gazette, 1/86 to present

(Portland) *Oregonian*, 1/89 to present

Richmond Times-Dispatch, 1/89 to present

Sacramento Bee, 1/88 to present

St. Louis Post Dispatch, 1/88 to present

Saint Paul Pioneer Press, 4/88 too present

St. Petersburg Times, 10/89 to present

San Francisco Chronicle, 1/88 to present

San Francisco Examiner, 6/90 to present

San Jose Mercury News, 6/85 to present

Seattle Post-Intelligencer, 1/90 to present

Seattle Times, 1/89 to present

USA Today, 1/88 to present

Washington Post, 4/83 to present

Washington Times, 1/89 to present

Wichita Eagle, 1/90 to present

See elsewhere in this book for newspapers available through other online vendors or on CD-ROMs.

For a complete listing of which newspapers are available online, see *Newspapers Online*. This directory includes information on nearly 200 daily North American and international newspapers, available online. It tells which online vendor includes which newspaper, with search tips for each. Check your library for this resource from BiblioData or call 1-617-444-

1154. Your local library should be able to tell you about access to your own newspaper online or on CD-ROM.

When you become part of Knight-Ridder Information DIALOG service, you will receive a list of approximately 450 databases, containing a veritable ocean of data. It has been estimated that it would take 2 million or so floppies to hold the information contained online. The poster-sized list of DIALOG databases is arranged alphabetically on one side, and by subject on the other.

From the subject guide, here are some of the categories, with examples of databases most used in nonprofit offices, with a short description of each from the DIALOG Catalogue.

BUSINESS & INDUSTRY

ABI/INFORM, File 15

This indexing and abstracting service to business journals also includes some full-text articles that can be sent via fax to subscribers.

BUSINESS DATELINE, File 635

This file contains the full text of selected articles from more than 350 American and Canadian local and regional business publications. Includes executive profiles.

TRADE & INDUSTRY INDEX, File 148

Information from business journals as relating to trade and industry are indexed with selective abstracts.

FINDEX, File 196

Market research reports and studies that are commercially available are indexed and described.

BUSINESS—BUSINESS STATISTICS

CENDATA, File 580

D&B - DONNELLEY DEMOGRAPHICS, File 575

POPULATION INDEX, File 581

These statistical databases use data from the 1980 and 1990 census from the Bureau of the Census, U.S. Department of Commerce, to give information on income, occupation, age, and education for geographical areas, down to individual ZIP codes. By asking for sorts, using income levels, one can find affluent ZIP codes in your city or elsewhere.

BUSINESS—INTERNATIONAL DIRECTORIES

D&B – INTERNATIONAL DUN'S MARKET IDENTIFIERS, File 518

D&B – CANADIAN DUN'S MARKET INDENTIFIERS, File 520

D&B – EUROPEAN DUN'S MARKET IDENTIFIERS, File 521

D&B – ASIA-PACIFIC DUN'S MARKET IDENTIFIERS, File 522

Foreign company information is available using these databases. The businesses represent all types of industries. Data is gathered from credit investigations and various third-party sources, such as government registrations.

BUSINESS—U.S. DIRECTORIES

FOUNDATION DIRECTORY, File 26

The Foundation Center in New York provides descriptions of more than 32,500 active grant makers. Information is from voluntary reports and from public information filed with the Internal Revenue Service.

FOUNDATION GRANTS INDEX, File 27

Also from the Foundation Center, this is an index to grants that were awarded to nonprofit organizations by over 800 foundations. The file is useful in determining types and amounts of grants awarded. It's updated quarterly with approximately 20,000 new grants each year.

GRANTS, File 85 (See under
MULTIDISCIPLINARY—REFERENCE, page
73.)

DISCLOSURE DATABASE, File 100

Derived from U.S. Securities and Exchange Commission (SEC) reports, this gives in-depth financial data on over 12,500 publicly owned companies.

STANDARD & POOR'S DAILY NEWS, File 132

General news and financial information on approximately 12,000 companies on major stock exchanges is updated daily for fast-breaking events such as mergers and management changes.

*STANDARD & POOR'S CORPORATE DESCRIP-
TIONS*, File 133

Basic company profiles are available here, with recent financial company news about earnings, subsidiaries, ratios, and balance sheet figures.

CORPORATE AFFILIATIONS, File 513

It tells who owns whom. The linkage between 100,000 companies worldwide is given, clearly showing parent and subsidiary companies.

D&B – DUN'S MARKET IDENTIFIERS, File 516

Because this includes over 7.5 million business establishments, this is a good place to begin a search for current address, product, financial, and marketing information. It includes private as well as public companies, and all product areas, so serves to identify less well-known companies.

D&B – MILLION DOLLAR DIRECTORY, File 517

Only the large companies are listed here, but it still includes 161,000 companies with sales of more than $25 million, more than 250 employees, or a net worth greater than $500,000. This includes private as well as public companies, with basic sales information.

D&B – DUN'S FINANCIAL RECORDS PLUS, File 519

Records go back three years for this database of historical and financial data. Beware: a full record can be very expensive. Check costs before printing or requesting full format.

STANDARD & POOR'S REGISTER – CORPORATE, File 527

Companies with sales over $1 million are given with basic information on address, a listing of officers and directors with their positions, and financial information. It includes both public and private companies.

AMERICAN BUSINESS DIRECTORY, File 531

National yellow pages are used to form this database, then the information is updated with yearly phone interviews. As with many of the business directories, one can get basic details on local businesses.

DISCLOSURE/SPECTRUM OWNERSHIP, File 540

This database is related to the DISCLOSURE file, but emphasizes public corporate ownership with stock holding information of major institutions, corporate insiders, and five-percent owners of 5,500 companies. Because emphasis is on ownership, this is often used by prospect researchers to determine an individual's net worth and relationship to a company.

SEC ONLINE:

    ANNUAL REPORTS, File 541

    10-K REPORTS, File 542

    10-Q REPORTS, File 543

    PROXY REPORTS, File 544

These four files come from SEC and are complete reports required by the SEC, as indicated by each file title. All are useful, but especially the 10-K and Proxy Reports as they give directors and executive officers with their annual compensation and stock ownership. Proxies often give biographical information networking the individual to other corporate or nonprofit boards.

INSIDER TRADING MONITOR, File 549

Insider trading filings of ownership changes received by the SEC are included here, from Invest/Net, a subcontractor to the SEC, that keeps track of ownership records for 100,000 officers and directors and major stockholders of over 8,500 public companies. It includes number of stocks bought or sold, price per share paid, and the insider's position in the company.

LAW AND GOVERNMENT

LEGAL RESOURCE INDEX, File 150

This provides cover-to-cover indexing of over 750 key law journals and legal newspapers. It's a good source to citations on ideas as expressed by legal professionals.

MULTIDISCIPLINARY — BOOKS

LC MARC BOOKS, File 426

If the individual you are researching has written a book, or been the subject of one, that was cataloged by the Library of Congress since 1968, it is listed in this database.

BOOKS IN PRINT, File 470

Is the book still in print and available from the publisher? This database gives the publishing record for the majority of books published in the United States, searchable by author, title, and subject with publisher addresses.

MULTIDISCIPLINARY — GENERAL INFORMATION

MAGAZINE INDEX, File 47

Covering 500 popular magazines, this index gives extensive access for current information on persons, companies and social issues. It is updated weekly and goes back to 1959 (with a break between 1970 and 1973.) Full-text articles can be displayed (but not searched word for word) for over 100 magazines.

MAGAZINE ASAP, File 647

This is connected to File 47, but it's somewhat different. This selectively provides complete text to over 100 publications in the above index. In this case, the full text is searchable, and the articles can be retrieved online.

MULTIDISCIPLINARY — REFERENCE

GRANTS, File 85

Most nonprofit organizations, at one time or another, are looking for grant support. Perhaps they are constantly searching. Online, grant seeking is somewhat easier than it had been. *GRANTS* is updated monthly and lists thousands of grants and scholarships offered by federal, state, and local governments; commercial organizations; associations; and private foundations.

Application information with deadlines are given with full description, qualifications, and grant amounts. *GRANTS* can be searched by subjects and by other qualifiers.

ENCYCLOPEDIA OF ASSOCIATIONS, File 114

This directory of over 88,000 nonprofit membership organizations worldwide is based on the classic print reference resource. It's useful because of its subject categories for all types of associations. It is a source for mailing lists of affinity groups or professional societies.

QUOTATIONS DATABASE, File 175

You've been asked to give a speech and you're looking for just the right quotation. Check this database for the perfect quote from literary and political classics. It's from the *Oxford Dictionary of Quotations*, with sources up to 1979.

MARQUIS WHO'S WHO, File 234

Another classic print-format resource has gone electronic and is all the better for it. Instead of searching several directories one after another, a researcher can get detailed biographies of over 82,000 individuals with career history, education, creative works, family background, current address, political activities and affiliation, religion, and special achievement. And you pay for just the names searched, not the whole database as when purchasing print editions.

BOWKER BIOGRAPHICAL DATABASE, File 236

More limited than the *MARQUIS WHO'S WHO* database, this is still useful if the names researched are from

NONPROFIT RESEARCHER OFF-LINE. — C.M.

specific fields. It's from the print versions of Bowker publications: *American Men and Women in Science*, *Who's Who in American Art*, and *Who's Who in American Politics*. It gives the same biographical data on each individual included.

BIOGRAPHY MASTER INDEX, File 287

This is one-stop shopping for biographical information. The index gives over 9.7 million citations for more than 3 million persons. It indexes current directories as well as retrospective dictionaries—more than 1,900 editions and volumes of 700 source publications. To distinguish one from the other, birth and death dates are given whenever possible, then the titles of books where biographical information can be found.

This corresponds to *Biography and Genealogy Master Index* and its annual updates in book format.

PUBLIC OPINION ONLINE (POLL), File 468

Have you wondered what public opinion thinks about a topic? Find out here. This database goes back to 1960 and covers the full spectrum of public interest surveys.

ULRICH'S INTERNATIONAL PERIODICAL DIRECTORY, File 480

With its complete access to titles of the world's periodicals, one can find what is available on every subject, even those very obscure irregular publications. Includes full bibliographic and ordering information.

STANDARD & POOR'S REGISTER — BIOGRAPHICAL, File 526

This database provides extensive personal and professional data on key executives and directors affiliated with both public and private companies, with sales of one million and more, and listed in the companion *STANDARD & POOR'S REGISTER – CORPORATE* database.

TIME PUBLICATIONS, File 746

This file includes the full text from popular magazines from Time, Inc., including *People*, *Fortune*, *Money*, *Sports Illustrated*, *Entertainment Weekly*, *Life*, and *Time*.

NEWS — NEWSPAPER INDEXES

NATIONAL NEWSPAPER INDEX, File 111

Quick access to major newspapers is available with this index. Useful if your research is for nationally known individuals.

> *Christian Science Monitor*, from 1979
>
> *New York Times*, from 1979
>
> *Wall Street Journal*, from 1979
>
> *Los Angeles Times*, from 1982
>
> *Washington Post*, from 1982.

NEWSEARCH, File 211

It's a daily index, but it archives only the current month. It indexes more than 2,000 news stories and articles in 1,700 newspapers, magazines, and journals, including many local business publications.

NEWSPAPER & PERIODICAL ABSTRACTS, File 484

Coverage for newspapers goes back to 1989 and to 1988 for periodicals. This huge database covers articles for over 26 newspapers and more than 1,500 periodicals.

NEWS —U.S. NEWSPAPERS FULL TEXT

See list on pages 63-64.

NEWS—WORLDWIDE NEWS

FINANCIAL TIMES FULL TEXT, File 622

The London and international editions of this very respected financial newspaper are available and useful for researching a company with an international perspective.

BUSINESS WIRE, File 610

PR NEWSWIRE, File 613

These two databases include news releases from companies, trade associations, public relations firms, etc. This is an important source of information on corporate donations and other charitable acts. As the files go back to 1986 and 1987, the history of a company can be traced through a compilation of its press releases.

TRADE & INDUSTRY INDEX

Articles on a wide range of topics make this worth checking for corporate information.

SOCIAL SCIENCES AND HUMANITIES

SOCIAL SCISEARCH, File 7

SOCIOLOGICAL ABSTRACTS, File 37

Both of these files are examples of multidisciplinary databases including either indexing to or abstracts from journals dealing with sociology or the social and behavioral sciences. As they cover original research, conference papers and dissertations, they can be very helpful for many current social interest research.

RELIGION INDEX, File 190

Aspects of most of the world's religions are featured in this index to over 500 journals.

BIBLE (KING JAMES VERSION), File 297

Okay, there may be better ways to read the Bible, but in a pinch, this can get you to the needed chapter and verse from the 1769 edition of both the Old and New Testaments.

Those databases listed above are just some of the DIALOG databases many nonprofit organizations will find very useful. You may discover others that meet your purposes even better. Although no one says that searching via online DIALOG is inexpensive, it may, indeed, be the most economical way to get the needed information. Because you can zero in on just what you need, rather than stagger through a great deal of information that is not relevant to your needs, you may actually save dollars.

Online, there is also the chance that you may find something that is available no other way. Who can put a price on some tidbit of information that leads to a grant or to a prospective donor?

Remember, you may be able to get the same information through Knowledge Index on CompuServe if you can search after business hours, between 6 p.m. and 5 a.m. your local time. Knowledge Index used to come directly from DIALOG, but since April 1993, it comes through CompuServe so it is more readily available to CompuServe subscribers, with no need for a separate DIALOG account.

Because DIALOG carved out its niche before CD-ROMs or before the Internet, it has developed very good technical support. Its range of available databases has something for everyone.

For several years DIALOG has been aware of its use in nonprofit development and research offices and has developed specific help for this market. Representatives have spoken at APRA's national conferences. Local chapters of that organization have sponsored DIALOG seminars. "Using DIALOG in the Development Office: Techniques, Databases, and Approaches for Utilizing Online Resources for Resource Development" is a DIALOG publication. Ask for a copy.

As stated, research done in development offices is usually for information about people, companies, foundations, and grants. "Using DIALOG in the Development Office" details some typical searches in each of those categories. Here is a summary of instructions on each search from that publication. It is not intended to tell exactly how to do a search. This is just a hint how it works for those who have never done an online search.

FINDING INFORMATION ON PEOPLE

To get basic biographical background, use the BIOGRAPH category that leads to biographical directories. It's a good idea to EXPAND to identify various ways the name may be written. That gives you a list of similar names, and you can choose all those that may be your person.

Pick some records from what seems to be the most complete database or with the most "hits" and type out the entry. For example, an entry from *Marquis Who's Who* database may be all you need for now. If not, proceed, being aware, of course, that all with the same name may not be the person you want.

Having the basic information, you may wish to continue and get information about the person's company, along with

You'll just have to wait. Our computer is online to DIALOG.

stock ownership, if he or she is an executive. Articles from the hometown daily and magazine articles may give personal information on your subject. This may be the most useful. Use DIALINDEX to cut to the chase, using these categories: PEOPLE, BIOGRAPH, PAPERS, NEWSWIRE, and REGIONAL. It tells you in which databases to find your answers.

If you have the name of a person, the search is fairly straightforward and the results are usually quite good.

Another sample challenge is to find business executives who went to a specific university and who live in your state. Here it is important to know which categories are searchable in, for example, *STANDARD & POOR'S REGISTER—BIOGRAPHICAL* database. Then, by searching for the university in the education field and the state in the address field, you will get those who fall into each category. Combine those two and you have your answer.

As you go along, you can see how the meter is ticking and see what the search is costing. You will learn techniques to save material to your hard disk to be printed later instead of while you are online. You can even "bail out" for a while to stop the clock, but save your search to that point. Go get a cup of coffee.

Instructions from DIALOG advise users to check the Bluesheets, giving specific details how each database works. They tell what fields are searchable by what commands. If you don't take that advice seriously, you will waste money.

FINDING INFORMATION ON COMPANIES

Because so many prospective donors come from the corporate world, it is not surprising that nonprofit researchers often seek information on both public and private companies. Luckily, there are many good databases available. The U.S. Securities and Exchange Commission was established in 1934 to protect the integrity of the securities system by requiring periodic reports from publicly owned companies. Thus, annual reports and proxy reports are good sources of information on the companies and their executive and directors.

Many company directories were most used for stock market transactions and other business purposes long before nonprofit organizations found this information also useful for their purposes. Business directories in book format are usually expensive. Most cost several hundred dollars each. You'll have to decide if you wish to use them at an academic or public library, go online and pay per search as you need the data, or buy the directories (realizing that next year there will be a new edition and it will cost even more). Depending on your needs, each may be best.

To do a company search you can use DIALINDEX categories: NEWSCO, USCO, PUBCO, INTLCO, REGIONAL, and TXTLN. EXPAND the company name to pick up all possibilities. If you want to know the major owners of a specific company, use DISCLOSURE SPECTRUM for shares held by insiders.

By using key words, it is possible to find lists of companies. For example, if you want a list of the largest companies in your area, use words such as "biggest" or "largest" plus the state, to narrow the search for magazine and newspaper articles.

You can get the already-published lists that way, but what if you want some lists that have not been compiled? With the SORT command, it is possible. From a list of companies in your state that gives sales amounts, sort from highest to lowest, and you have your list.

FINDING DEMOGRAPHIC INFORMATION

Nonprofit organizations have many reasons to search for demographic data, whether by state, city, neighborhood, or ZIP code. Using that same data-sorting command, you can, for example, find the ZIP codes in your city with the wealthiest per capita household income. Finding these neighborhoods is a question often asked of prospect researchers as an organization begins a major campaign. Conversely, if an agency is doing social analysis or seeking logical sites for service locations, they may seek areas with low income levels.

Most information in demographic files was gathered by the U.S. Census Bureau during regular censuses. Then it is made available in either *CENDATA* or *POPULATION DEMOGRAPHICS* files on DIALOG.

FINDING FOUNDATION AND GRANTS INFORMATION

Whether it's from corporations, local or federal government, foundations, or individuals, the purpose of most research done by development offices is to identify sources of support. It's what keeps the organization going.

Databases called *FOUNDATION GRANTS INDEX*, *FOUNDATION DIRECTORY*, and *GRANTS*, all available on DIALOG, are good places to begin research for those ever-needed funds.

Using *GRANTS*, define the terms of the programs for which you wish to obtain a grant, then use that term to call up the possible grants to support that program. As the search extracts descriptor words, it is for the researcher to match those that apply and call up the main entry for the grant.

Knowing which grants have been given to what types of organizations is a useful guide to those for which you may wish to apply.

Another classic, the *FOUNDATION DIRECTORY*, existed for years as the main source of foundation grant information. Now in electronic format, it is even more useful and easier to use. Rather than the rather tedious task of checking the print index, then looking for the correct page number, now the computer does the sorting for you. You can get your main targets with greater precision.

Using DIALOG to search Foundation Center databases will be easier with the use of a new *DIALOG User Manual and Thesaurus*, published by the Foundation Center. The manual shows how to retrieve facts quickly and easily from the Foundation Center's database on foundation and corporate grant makers. Keep it by your desk and use it before beginning each search.

DIALOG suggests using press release databases as part of your grant search. Once you have identified a few grants, check if more information is available from corporate or foundation releases from when previous grants were awarded.

OTHER DIALOG SERVICES

It's time consuming, and it can be expensive, to keep searching for that proverbial tidbit of information in the electronic universe. DIALOG can do it for you with its Alert service. It allows you to select the topics or persons you are researching, then pick the databases to be checked automatically. When a "hit" is found, you get a copy by Internet e-mail, fax, DIALOG Dialmail, or first class mail. Whichever you wish.

DIALOG can set up customized ART accounts, designed for the type of searching you do most often. For faxed information on this, or any DIALOG service, call 1-800-496-4470 for As Soon as Faxable (ASAF) instant access to information. Request Index 1000 to see what is available, then request up to five documents per call. It is faxed to you within minutes of your request.

What good is knowing the citation of an article if you don't have access to the actual article? KR SourceOne (formerly DIALOG SourceOne) provides copies via mail, fax, or e-mail of the needed article from their digital image collection of ABI/INFORM or documents from other sources.

Don't try to remember everything that is available from Knight-Ridder Information DIALOG. It's too overwhelming. If you are a beginner, start slowly, picking up expertise and speed as you go along.

6

Online by Direct Access: Something for Everyone

"The secret to business is to know something that nobody else knows."

Aristotle Onassis

Many different subject databases are available through an "umbrella" vendor such as Knight-Ridder Information DIALOG, which also makes many databases available through Knowledge Index from CompuServe. Others, such as DataTimes, include databases from hundreds of newspapers, by direct hookup to DataTimes. Others are direct access, meaning you can dial directly into the company that produces the database. Here are several other online information providers.

FOR NEWSPAPER ARTICLES AND LEGAL DOCUMENTS

DATATIMES

DataTimes is a direct-dial online service giving full-text access to over 100 major metropolitan daily newspapers from all 50 states and the District of Columbia with same-day access to regional business news from more than 140 newspapers. Do you need information from international newspapers? They are here.

Searching full-text newspapers for names of persons or companies used to be hard. Impossible, really, until newspapers began to be published electronically, making it possible to access every word. Before that, a print index would contain general subject indexing, article by article, not word by word. Humans decided under what subject an article should be put, and, unless a person was a principal in the article, no entry was made. Then, as if by magic, electronic publishing developed. The computer can match words, letter by letter. It can pick out the word in relation to others close by. Say you want John Johnson, one of many so named in the database. Match it with the ABC Company and you get a hit for just that John Johnson, if his company is mentioned.

If you are looking for a person or company with mention of charitable interests, you can match the name with other possible terms to get a match, if one exists. Because most searches are name by name, full-text searching is relatively straightforward. With DataTimes, pick the paper you wish to search and continue from there, with easy instructions. Some researchers use both DIALOG and DataTimes in tandem. They use, for example, an index on DIALOG, then get the full text here.

The advent of Macintosh, and then Windows, with click-on icons made gateway software to online services easier. DataTimes offers graphics with "EyeQ" for Windows users and "DataTimes Online" for those using DOS. Some prefer the faster "old" way to access DataTimes because the information came directly from the database, not reformatted through Eye-Q to fit the Windows format. Call 1-800-642-2525 or 1-405-751-6400 for a free starter kit and for additional information.

Besides the newspaper access, DataTimes includes online business and company information. Many of the basic Standard & Poor's reports, credit reports, annual reports, and company profiles are here. Executive reports cost between $25 and $35, sent online, by fax, or by regular mail.

DataTimes pricing is customized, based on actual and projected usage patterns. According to the company, flat fees are negotiated individually and offer users the ability to budget more effectively. There is also a pay-as-you-go schedule, with a monthly fee of $59. Searching is then free, but there are viewing, printing, or downloading fees. The researcher can get a citation to headline, date and source, but full-text documents cost $3 each. Other choices are KWIC (Key Word or Words in Context) or lead paragraph of a document.

Another feature, though I'm not sure how much this is used, are full transcripts to 100 top television news programs. Included are "60 Minutes," "Today," "Larry King Live," "Inside Business," and "Meet the Press." Radio transcripts are from National Public Radio.

LEXIS-NEXIS

LEXIS-NEXIS pioneered electronic full-text access service to many of the leading legal, news, and business information sources.

It began as LEXIS in 1973, as the first commercial full-text legal information service to help legal professionals research the law more efficiently. Then, few offices had their own computers, so LEXIS provided a custom terminal and printer to its subscribers.

LEXIS contains major archives of federal and state case law, with continual updating from all 50 states. Perhaps in no other field is full text more important than law. Subscribers to LEXIS have access to NEXIS.

The NEXIS service began in 1979 as a full-text news and business information service, now with over 2,400 full-text sources. It's the exclusive online archival source for the *New York Times* to the legal, business, and other professional markets. It also carries other major news publications, including the *Washington Post, Los Angeles Times, Business Week, Fortune,* and *The Economist.* It abstracts the *Wall Street Journal.*

For your nonprofit office, depending on your needs, you will probably use NEXIS more than LEXIS, unless your organization does some legal research, needing case law documentation. If so, you can be sure your attorney knows about LEXIS and probably has it in her or his office. Any attorney trained since 1973 will have used LEXIS during law school and will not imagine how they could survive without it.

Currently, many, if not most, college and university libraries offer LEXIS-NEXIS access to their students for their course work. What better way to hook those entering the professional markets on a service they will need later? It works. Ask new professionals, in almost any field, what online service they would like, the answer probably will be this one. There's only one catch. While in school the students got free access while doing class work. Out in the real world, it costs. A lot. Minute by minute, the dollars tick away.

While this is true of all online services, LEXIS-NEXIS has the reputation of an expensive resource, but if you can quickly get what you need, it's worth it.

Your development office, as part of a college or university, may be able to access this online service through the campus library. Others, in large organizations fortunate enough to have a research library, may be able to become part of a local-area network accessing LEXIS-NEXIS.

Perhaps the most useful NEXIS access is to regional business newspapers. As nonprofit organization staffs research individuals and corporations capable of making significant donations, these regional sources are most apt to tell about those local persons (many are company executives) with information about the companies. An example of useful data is on political campaign giving, available in the CAMPAIGN NEWS library on LEXIS-NEXIS. This includes both federal and state campaigns.

Files in NEXIS are located in libraries. Thus, most of the regional newspapers are in the NEWS library with BUSDTL as its file name. That's the "home" library but often access can be made through other routes. Here is just a sampling of the regional newspapers or journals available online through NEXIS. They cover every part of the country.

Alaska Business Monthly, Arizona Business Gazette, Birmingham Business Journal, Colorado Springs Business Journal, Duluthian, Georgia Trend, Lehigh Valley Business Digest, New Miami, Peoria Journal Star, San Antonio Light, Toledo Business Journal, and *Westchester County Business Journal.*

Well, you get the idea. Multiply that by hundreds and you get the scope of regional newspaper coverage in NEXIS.

That's just in this country. Now add the world for a bigger picture. In the library called WORLD, there are publications and wire services from each continent. Examples: *Singapore Business Times, Eastern Europe Reports, Jerusalem Post, Moscow News, Latin American Newsletters, Predicasts Asian & Pacific Rim Information,* and the *Vancouver Sun.* There are hundreds more.

Both *Forbes* and *Fortune* magazines are in the MARKET library, along with dozens of business, financial, and general publications. The *Federal Register* is in the LEGIS library, for those following government legislation or looking for newly announced federal grants.

Realizing that research about people, for all kinds of reasons, is crucial, NEXIS has a PEOPLE library. Included here are *The Almanac of American Politics, Directory of Bankruptcy Attorneys* (okay, you never know when you might need that), *Gale Biographies, Los Angeles Times Biographical Stories,* the *Washington Post Biographical Stories,* and *New York Times Biographical File* and the *New York Times Biographical File – Government,* and *People Magazine.* The classic *Martindale–Hubbell Law Directory Practice Profiles* is here, for your research on an American attorney.

The ASSETS library includes aircraft and boat registrations for the entire country. Check who is zooming into the local airport on those Lear jets. Real estate records include property owners, how much they paid for the property, and information about the mortgage.

You can use the ENTERT library in NEXIS to find information on celebrities. Look for biographies or profiles of corporate leaders, plus news about others involved in the entertainment industry. The CONTCS file is searchable by celebrity name and will usually, at least, get you a way to contact the person's agent or manager.

In the BUSREF library, under the file name of GQUOTE is the *3,500 Good Quotes for Speakers.* It has that many quotes of concise and humorous statements "reflecting the imperfection of human behavior." It is indexed by subject and source and includes the complete text of the quote.

A very useful feature of NEXIS is SEC reports. The COMPANY library includes the most popular filings.

Special services are available from LEXIS-NEXIS. For the faint of heart who would rather pay someone else to do the search, that is possible—for a price. It's called NEXIS EXPRESS, and the only electronic equipment you need is your telephone. No computer, no modem, just your telephone. Anybody can subscribe to LEXIS-NEXIS but not all have the staff, or the inclination, to do their own research.

Here's how it works, from the LEXIS-NEXIS brochure. "You call our toll-free 800 number (1-800-843-6476) and tell us what you need to know. Something for a project you're working on; something you'll need for a presentation a day from now; some bit of information you vaguely remember hearing someone say, somewhere. Next, we may ask some questions to help you define exactly what it is you're looking for. We may even suggest other questions you may not have thought of. Then you go back to your work, and we go to work to get comprehensive results."

The results are delivered by fax, overnight delivery, or regular mail. The cost depends on the time it took to do the job. (You'll get an estimate before they start.) What it will cost depends on the complexity of the search, but the average search costs between $30 and $100, averaging $6 per minute. It's not for everyone, but if a major contribution depends on your knowing something about the donor, this may be well worth it. And it is less stressful than doing the research yourself, if you have only occasional need for such information. The fee is charged on a credit card.

A useful feature with LEXIS-NEXIS is ECLIPSE, an electronic "clipping service," that will search, on a regular basis, for information on the subject or person you want. It compares to DIALOG Alert. Either will notify you when new documents that meet your requirements are found, after you save a search request and lock into the ECLIPSE system. It usually is less expensive than starting a new search each time you want to check on new material. What it costs depends on your subscription terms.

According to information from LEXIS-NEXIS, pricing is highly customized for different customer groups due to their varying needs. Pricing falls into three basic categories: subscription, hourly, and transactional. It varies by anticipated or past use and which databases are used. To get you started, there is an infrequent user plan.

The multimillion-dollar computer center in Dayton, Ohio, is connected to leased high-speed circuits to thousands of subscribers' terminals via the LEXIS-NEXIS network. Subscribers receive special research software with formats for Windows and Macintosh environments. Connection can also be through commercial networks with the basic personal computer equipped with a communications modem.

For a packet of information on the services, plus a catalog of databases, call 1-800-227-4908 or 1-513-859-1608.

DOW JONES NEWS/RETRIEVAL

Dow Jones has been publishing information for and about businesses for over a century. It, like other publishers, began putting words on paper. In this information age, it provides several services online. It offers full text to the *Wall Street Journal* and hundreds of other publications, including the *Washington Post*, the *Los Angeles Times,* and *New York Times* abstracts. It is continually adding new papers, including many regional and international ones.

It promises a library of 1,750 information sources from business and the financial world. You can access this information from your computer, equipped with a modem, after you establish an account and get a Dow Jones password. Dow Jones News Service and its international version provide continually updated news coverage.

The Business Dateline file includes profiles of CEOs, boards of directors, entrepreneurs, and managers as part of its full-text coverage of business issues.

Dow Jones has a Clip feature to automatically locate news on subjects you choose. For example, make a file for a company or individual you are researching and the incoming news is scanned for you. Then, the found information is e-mailed or faxed to you.

Besides access to news stories, Dow Jones provides business and financial data on both private and public companies, including *D&B Dun's Market Identifiers* and *Standard & Poor's Online. SEC Online* gives access to most SEC company reports.

While most other online services provide information by number of minutes online, Dow Jones charges at a rate of $1.50 per 1,000 characters, plus a special fee, in most cases, depending on which report is requested. (Caution: characters are often hidden. They are the letters and numbers you see, but also the spaces between words and paragraphs. Those unseen characters add up, like calories in a piece of chocolate cake — unseen, but there.)

The service is online 24 hours a day, and its customer service assumes you may work late. It's available until midnight Monday through Friday and until 6 on Saturday (all eastern time).

Call 1-800-815-5100 for a packet of information and to request free usage to begin service.

DOW JONES "PERSONAL JOURNAL"

It is debatable whether people will like to read newspapers or magazines online. Several are now available through the commercial online services, for example, *U.S. News and World Report* on CompuServe. Parts of the daily *New York Times* are on America Online, but there is no archival access.

The first week of March 1995, an offshoot of the *Wall Street Journal* became available to nationwide subscribers online. It is called the *Dow Jones Personal Journal* and, to quote the advertising, is "Published for a circulation of one." For a monthly subscription fee of $12.95 for one edition every business day, a person can dial directly to Dow Jones. Rather than stay online to read it, the publication can be downloaded to a hard disk, on either a laptop or desktop computer. Downloading takes about three minutes with a 9,600-baud modem. The reader then can browse through the articles as needed, clicking on icons for specific columns and articles.

Rather than being a complete daily *Wall Street Journal*, the *Personal Journal* can, indeed, be personalized. When subscribing, the reader is asked to complete a reader profile, designating desired columns, companies he or she wishes to track, and subjects of interest. Then, should an article on the designated company appear, it will become part of a subscriber's *Personal Journal*. For an additional 50 cents per time, an afternoon update can be checked.

Whether this catches on remains to be seen. Access to newspapers for research is best if there is an archive going back several years, so one can search for names of persons and companies. Reading a newspaper, the *Wall Street Journal* or any other, is most often a serendipitous experience. You spot things of interest, far beyond what you are looking for. Any subject may catch the eye and be of interest. That's harder to do online.

Call Dow Jones at 1-800-291-9382, ext. 984, for information on the *Personal Journal* for a free two-week subscription.

BRS

BRS offers about 145 databases on most subjects, with strong emphasis on medical-related databases. While the databases will probably not be the most used, BRS does include the Wilsonline databases that are good for periodical indexes.

Like Knowledge Index, BRS has an off-hours option called BRS/AfterDark, when about 90 databases are less expensive. ABI/INFORM, a periodical index with many business periodicals included is here and useful for its well-written abstracts.

Call BRS at 1-800-289-4277

PROFOUND

The "new kid on the block" for online business intelligence is *Profound*, introduced late spring 1995, designed to compete with NEXIS. It offers full documents, with pictures and graphics, from over 4,000 newspapers, periodicals, and news wires, plus short or full-text corporate research reports of various origins, at various costs. A Custom Alert feature will check for a customer's designated terms or names.

Charges begin at $19.95 per month, with hourly connection time at $6.95. There are charges for documents and articles read or retrieved. When the service began, it required a credit card number with application. That can be difficult for some nonprofits that prefer monthly billing, rather than automatic billing to a credit card. As with most online services, there is an introductory offer of free software and five free online hours available from 1-800-851-1229 or 1-800-638-7139 or 1-212-447-6900.

STOCK OWNERSHIP

While determining, or estimating, net worth for a prospect or donor, it is very useful to know whether that person is an insider or major stockholder in a company. While that information may be available for individual companies, from their proxy statements, it is nice to have a collective picture of a person's stock holdings. It is available online and matched with other data to enhance its value.

CDA INVESTNET

CDA Investnet can provide a financial profile matching SEC reports of stock ownership for public company officers, directors, and beneficial owners that are on file with the Securities and Exchange Commission. With its "Insider Trading Monitor," the company uses a name and address supplied from the client to match collected data that can show indications of wealth. The result will show stock holdings in all companies where the person is an insider, current market value of stock, dividends earned, ten years of stock sales, and trade dates.

Then, with a CDA service called FACT$ (Factual And Comprehensive Targeting Solutions,) that name can be matched with CD-ROM databases from Taft giving further biographical and philanthropic information. That will show where to locate personal and family information, past charitable gifts, and "who knows whom" from corporate and nonprofit directorships. A further match will show real estate holdings and household demographic indications of wealth.

While there are other companies designed to pinpoint major donors, CDA Investnet is one that has grown in the last several years to understand the type of data needed by nonprofit executives and has known where to find it. Then, it has packaged the information for convenient direct online access. In 1992 The Invest/Net Group was acquired by CDA/Investment Technologies, Inc., and became part of Thomson Financial Service, a large Toronto-based public company. As part of that company, *CDA Investnet* was able to lock into vast databases of public information.

A 1994 APRA survey of those who used electronic databases indicated that 21.5 percent had used Investnet for financial information. Call 1-800-933-4446 or 1-305-384-1500 and ask CDA Investnet for an information packet. Once you get the pricing details for your size organization you can determine if this in-depth analysis of your prospects and donors will be useful.

To find other companies that offer donor matching services, check the display advertising in nonprofit publications and look for product demonstrations at fund-raising and research conferences. Each month, it seems, more companies develop software services for nonprofit donor management.

BUSINESS INFORMATION — ONLINE

AMERICAN BUSINESS INFORMATION

If you know only the name of a company but have no clue where it is, *American Business Information* may be a good place to begin searching for information on it. Online, paying just for what you need, may be less costly than other business databases. This may give you just enough to get your research started.

About 10 million U.S. and 1 million Canadian businesses are compiled from telephone yellow pages, so you may get several companies with the same name, but getting the locations may help pinpoint the one you need. Online it's available 24 hours a day.

American Business Information costs $95 for an annual subscription with each online search costing $1 per minute and 25 cents to display the information.

Call for details at 1-402-592-9000.

So what happens when you want business information but you are not near your computer or have never taken the step to hook your PC to a modem to reach the outside world? Well, American Business Information, Inc., can take care of you via the old-fashioned telephone. Call their INFO ACCESS service at 1-800-808-4636. Seven services are provided: company profiles, business credit reports, business directory assistance, "Find-a-Person" (track down a friend, a prospect, or a business colleague), quick research service, business news network, and legal information network. Answers come by telephone or fax.

There is an annual $45 membership fee, then other services are charged as used, but beginning with $50 free usage. It's available only weekdays between 7 a.m. to 6 p.m. central standard time.

BLOOMBERG BUSINESS NEWS

BLOOMBERG BUSINESS NEWS covers governments, corporations, industries, and all financial markets around the world. As such, it has become a prime source of news for U.S. newspapers. Check your big-city newspaper and you will probably see a Bloomberg byline on the business pages.

This service comes on a dedicated computer terminal called—guess what?—the BLOOMBERG. It alerts the user to breaking news and developments in the stock markets. For those who need information quickly, this service succeeds very well. But it is known as an expensive database, so it may not be the first choice to get needed financial information for nonprofit staffs.

As the owner of the "world's fastest growing business news and information service," Michael Bloomberg is said to have a personal fortune of at least $1 billion and is generous with it. In October 1995, he donated $55 million to his alma mater, Johns Hopkins University in Baltimore. As head of the university's fund-raising campaign, he said when he accepted the position he would have to give a major donation to "lead by example." All nonprofit organizations applauded!

Call Bloomberg at 1-212-318-2000.

REAL ESTATE INFORMATION

There are several reasons why nonprofit organizations may need information on the value of real estate. When doing prospect research, the value of a prospect's or donor's home or other property may help determine a person's net worth. If the gift of real estate becomes an offer, it helps to know its value. Or, when negotiating to purchase office or other-use property, it helps to know neighborhood values. Although your real estate agent can, most often, supply such information, sometimes it helps to be able to get such data yourself.

TRW REDI

Several online data companies offer help. One is *TRW REDI*. Although property values have been available through assessor offices and through print directories in many metropolitan areas, now online access makes this easier and accessible in your own office, through your computer.

TRW REDI gathers and makes available information on over 50 million real estate parcels nationwide. To quote their fact sheet, "The lineage of *TRW REDI* property data stretches back for more than fifty years and includes former companies such as TRW Real Estate Information Services, REDI Real Estate Information Services, Lusk, and DAMAR."

The databases contain the names of people who own properties, the dates the properties were purchased, and at what price. The physical characteristics of the property are included. The primary use of such databases is for real estate professionals so they can price homes, estimate their market value, and confirm whether or not properties may be sold.

Data is gathered from more than 300 county and municipal government offices in 34 states. The Home Price Index is available in 40 states nationwide. *TRW REDI* offers a choice for accessing the files online to those with an annual subscription agreement. The same data is available on CD-ROM, updated each month.

Even if your office does not have enough use for such a service to justify an annual subscription, it is helpful to know real estate online services exist. Public libraries (try the local history room for hometown information), real estate brokerages, and mortgage bankers may be able to help get the real estate information you need.

Call 1-800-345-7334 or 1-800-421-1052 for price information on the services and to see if your locality is included in one of the *TRW REDI* products and services.

DATAQUICK

DataQuick has 16 databases, some for marketing by providing demographic-specific lists, and others for research. The Real Estate Data files provide sale/loan, ownership, and assessment information on property in California and metropolitan areas of Arizona, Nevada, Oregon, and Washington. For each property listed, it gives owner's name, name of spouse, second owner name, mailing address, site address, county assessor's parcel number, and assessed value.

Some of their online services include national databases. Such is *PeopleTracker* that can be searched by name, for $30 per report, and phone number, for $15 per report. If no records are found, the charge is $3. The research database includes 100 million names and gives address, age, median income, and a neighborhood listing. Prices per real estate search vary. There is a one-time account establishment fee of $200 and a minimum monthly fee of $50. That fee applies against all charges and includes access to all online services. Online access surcharges per minute depend on the client's computer baud rate. *DataQuick* services are available as hardcopy products, on microfiche, and on CD-ROM. For more information on the wide range of services from *DataQuick*, call the national sales office at 1-800-863-4636 or the corporate offices at 1-619-455-6900 for regional numbers for the western states.

Real Estate MATCH from *CDA Investnet* provides real estate holdings for wealthy individuals online. It matches names against 36 million residential properties in over 580 counties across America. Basic data can be found: purchase price, assessed value, property description, current market value, mortgage, and geographical comparisons. This, matched with other databases from the same company, can give important net worth estimates. Call *CDA Investnet* at 1-800-933-4446 or 1-305-384-1500 for an information packet.

DAMAR REAL ESTATE INFORMATION SERVICE

This is an online database that covers properties, mostly those in California, but also areas in Arizona and Illinois. It describes real estate with sales and mortgage prices. One file is national in scope, containing information on significant U.S. commercial and industrial real estate sales transactions.

Call 1-800-345-7334.

CONSUMER REPORTS HOME PRICE SERVICE

Because we are all curious about what friends paid for a house or what our own house is now worth by using neighborhood "comparable," Consumers Union started this service in July 1995 giving the answers to those questions. It doesn't even require a computer. Just a touch-tone telephone. Nonprofits may decide this is the least expensive, most convenient way to get real estate prices for reasons mentioned above.

With *Consumer Reports Home Price Service*, a nationwide resource, from nonprofit Consumers Union, publisher of *Con-*

sumer Reports magazine, real estate information is open to subscribers and nonsubscribers.

By using a credit card number and responding to a series of prompts, you can pick the state you want to research, then the town. At that point you can either check out a specific address, check for sales along an entire street, or survey sales within a range of a maximum price. The database of sales stretches back five to six years in most areas and has 24-hour access.

By the time you read this, bugs should be worked out and the service may be very helpful for the limited real estate information needed by nonprofit staffs. Call 1-800-775-1212.

The cost is just $10 for 10 minutes, covering prices of up to 24 houses, plus a fax printout sent to you at no additional cost within a minute or two of hanging up. Wow!

THE ENTERTAINMENT INDUSTRY

BASELINE

Baseline contains information on the U.S. entertainment industry, with an emphasis on films, television, and theater. A Names (NMS) file gives biographical information on more than 300,000 creative, technical, and administrative personnel in the industry, beginning with 1970.

A Bio section is about celebrities, and a Contacts (CON) section tells how to contact more than 10,000 of them, giving the agent's name.

Baseline is available on a one-time subscription basis plus usage fees. Call 1-800-242-7546 or 1-212-254-8235 for more details.

FOR GOVERNMENT AND OTHER GRANTS

FAPRS

FAPRS stands for the Federal Assistance Programs Retrieval System. It is the online version of the *Catalog of Domestic Federal Assistance* from the General Services Administration.

It tells what federal programs are available, eligibility requirements, examples of funded projects, and how to apply. The online version gives keyword and category searches to that resource.

With your personal computer and a modem with communications software, you can subscribe for an annual fee of $50. Then you can scan the database, looking for federal grants to fit. Diskette or CD-ROM versions are available for this product, (see Chapter 3) but you may prefer this online route. It includes on-line definitions of categories with extensive help from *FAPRS* staff at this electronic bulletin board. Because it is online, it includes a monthly "News" section with abstracts from the *Federal Register* as they relate to grants and assistance programs.

Call 1-202-708-5126 to order or get more information.

THE FOUNDATION CENTER ASSOCIATES PROGRAM

The Foundation Center has long been the prime depository for foundation information and the publisher of the much-used *Foundation Directory*. It offers an experienced fund-raising researcher at the end of a telephone or fax line to its Associates Program. For an annual membership fee of $495, subscribers can make ten reference calls per month and get information from the Center's resources. There are additional photocopy, fax, and customized computer search charges.

If your resource library is limited, this is an excellent way to let an expert search for grants for your organization. For example, if your foundation grant search is done only once or twice a year, it may be less expensive to use the Associates Program rather than purchase the directories of foundations. (You can find those for use at most libraries. Or you can search for grants online, as described elsewhere in this book.)

Call the Foundation Center at 1-800-424-9836 for details on the Associates Program. Also, ask for a free catalog of their publications.

SPIN Online (Sponsored Programs Information Network Database) gives information on over 5,600 U.S. federal government, nonfederal, and corporate sources of funding for research, education, and development projects. Especially for educational institutions, this includes funding for fellowships, postdoctoral opportunities, and publication support. This is also available on a diskette.

Call InfoEd (Information for Education) at 1-518-464-0691.

NONPROFIT DONET OF GEORGIA

DoNet is a fee-based, computerized online service from the Atlanta fund-raising firm Alexander O'Neill Haas & Martin. It is designed specially for fund-raising executives in Georgia, with plans to expand to other southeastern states later. It provides philanthropic information on foundations, corporations, and individuals in Georgia, searchable by keyword or name. Philanthropic news stories, foundation and corporate reports, and grant information are added daily.

Because this is limited geographically, it can provide a wider range of data than a service that tries to be national in scope. Call 1-800-490-8039 or 1-404-875-7575 for pricing information and instructions for a trial "tour" of *DoNet* databases.

FOR NEWSLETTERS

NewsNet is a database offering direct access to about 800 industry newsletters and other publications. It is possible to subscribe to it directly, or, it is available on CompuServe through the IQuest service. Either way, it offers quick, hot-off-the-press news that may be available in newsletters before appearing in other periodicals.

Examples of publications included are: *Foundation Giving Watch; Federal Grants and Contracts Weekly; Health Grants and Contracts Weekly;* and *Nonprofit Insights*.

It offers a SEARCH feature where you pinpoint the information of most interest, using keywords. Those keywords, used in connection with AND or OR, plus basic online search techniques, then lead directly to the needed information from the newsletters.

Perhaps best of all, *NewsNet* has a NewsFlash option, an electronic clipping service geared to your needs. You create a folder according to your needs and tell *NewsNet* to look for articles on that subject, then stash them into your folder. If, for example, your nonprofit organization is health care related, you could have NewsFlash look for items about that industry.

The next time you log on, *NewsNet* tells you how many new hits there are in your folder. You can choose to display them by headline, full text, or with keyword analysis.

The subscription fee is $120 per year, or $15 per month. The basic connect charge is 25 cents per minute throughout all sessions. An information retrieval rate of $1.50 per minute applies when displaying headlines or full text or for premium gateway services offered by NewsNet.

The best way to decide if this database service has what you need is to call 1-800-952-0122 or 1-527-8030 for an information packet. See what newsletters are included and how they relate to your needs.

POLITICAL CONTRIBUTIONS

FEDERAL ELECTION COMMISSION

Within the federal government, the agency in charge of keeping elections honest and letting citizens know who gets how much from whom is the Federal Election Commission. Their collected information is available as an inexpensive on-line system, called *FEC Direct Access Program (DAP)*. For nonprofits, the most interesting part deals with contributions by individuals to political candidates, political action committees, and political parties. This federal information, however, is for information only, not to be used for commercial or solicitation purposes.

Development offices for nonprofit organizations can use this service to assist in a prospect profile. Knowing a person's political inclination is one clue to that person's identity and may indicate concerns and interests. FEC's computerized information is derived from actual disclosure reports filed by political committees. Thus, you can do a global search that will turn up contributions made in a person's name. Disclosure includes place of business or occupation, city and state, and date of contribution. It's offered, thanks to Freedom of Information legislation.

You can get detailed information on this database by fax by dialing 1-202-501-3413 and requesting document number 306. It tells the procedure for prepaying for the online service at a rate of $20 per usage hour. Once you decide to subscribe and send in your check, service is available in about 10 days, and you get a user handbook to help you navigate the menu-driven system. For other information, call 1-800-424-9530.

Most states provide networks for local campaign data. Ask your state elections office to see what is available in your locality. For example, California has State Net, an online service telling what is going on in state government. As mentioned, LEXIS-NEXIS includes regional campaign contributions.

SEARCHING FOR INDIVIDUALS (AND PUBLIC RECORDS ABOUT THEM)

Once telephone directory databases for the complete country were available in one alphabetical list, searchable by name with qualifiers such as city or state, it was a fairly simple thing to offer online access to those databases as a way to local "lost" alumni, past donors who have moved away, or potential prospects.

Some nonprofit organizations have chosen to purchase telephone directories on CD-ROMs (discussed in Chapter 2) to do their own searching for those who have strayed. Others use PhoneFile online through CompuServe. When searching between 70 and 80 million records, one can hope the name searched is very unusual. To understand the magnitude of the problem, check your own directory for Smith or Lee, then imagine having every phone book in one alphabetical listing!

Two databases from Information America, *Executive Affiliations* and *People Finder*, profile individuals. The first promises to link executives to all the business concerns with which they may be listed as a principal or officer. The second gives household information, including family name, address, telephone number, residence type, length of residence, family members, birth dates, and up to ten neighbors with addresses and telephone numbers.

Costs vary, depending on how wide an area is searched, so call 1-800-235-4008 or 1-404-892-1800.

PC411

Others looking for a "lost" person can do a search with an online connection from *PC411*. Windows software is available for $49.95 that includes a $15 usage credit. It is accessible at any hour. Once online, the user can access the database, instead of calling a phone company 411 or long-distance information operator. Using *PC411* for hourly usage charges requires a major credit card.

Call PC411 at 1-800-2-GET-411 for details.

Getting the telephone number and address for a person is quite simple; after all, most persons are listed in the local telephone directory. But many aren't. In most cases, those persons will not turn up in the electronic directories either.

Public Records

What is also available, and a bit disturbing, is a virtual shopping list of a person's entire life story, gleaned from public records and put into databases that can be zapped around the country electronically. Not only *can* be—but *are* zapped around, at an estimated rate of 5 billion records a day. It has been estimated that information on each of us is moved from computer to another computer about five times each day!

Depending on which side of information gathering you are on, you may be amazed at all the information that is available to you. When you realize the same information is available *about* you, you may be less enchanted with such research possibilities. Privacy advocates are horrified that personal information keeps getting sold, resold, and sold again. Such data has become a commodity. It's probably easier to stop a computer virus than to stop the route of data available online on any individual.

Personnel directors, law enforcement officers, private investigators, journalists, mortgage bankers, credit bureaus, attorneys, and marketers were among the first to use this collected information on individuals. Now, for better or worse, there is no limit to those using the data.

Fund raisers, prospect researchers, and nonprofit executives have long been concerned about privacy violation in their research. Organizations such as the Association of Professional

An idea of what public records are available was discussed in *Home Office Computing,* June 1995. Here's a "Snooper's Checklist," a listing of what online services may be disclosing about you. Surprisingly, all the information is from public records.

- Your name
- Your age
- Who lives with you
- The ages of your spouse and children
- How much your house is worth
- Who co-owns your house
- Who you bought your house from
- When you bought your house and what size or type of dwelling it is
- Your neighbors' addresses and telephone numbers
- What you earn (a close approximation)
- Whether you've been incarcerated and for what reason

Researchers for Advancement, the National Society of Fund Raising Executives, the American Association of Fund-Raising Counsel, and Council for Advancement and Support of Education (CASE) each have a code of ethics dealing with privacy issues.

It is not my intention to detail what should be collected for what type of office, except to say privacy is an issue that must be discussed in all types of nonprofit offices. Each organization should have a clear analysis of what to research—then how and why.

It should also be pointed out that some companies that provide credit reports now are more readily accessible than previously. Using those services, if only for address verification,

---

- Whether there are any federal or state tax liens against you
- Your creditors
- The collateral for any outstanding loans
- Your real estate holdings
- Whether you also do business under another name (including a fictious one)
- Whether your corporation is in good standing
- The information in corporate forms you have filed with state officials
- Your property tax bill
- Whether you've violated environmental regulations
- Whether you've filed for bankruptcy
- If you've owned property that was foreclosed
- Your divorce record
- If you've sued or been sued
- If there are judgments against you.

ENOUGH ALREADY!!!

---

can create problems. Some nonprofits have reported getting calls from donors or friends indicating their institution was listed as having requested reports. Be aware of the questions your donors may ask about this.

This book gives some (but not all) sources for different types of information, not to recommend what should or should not be researched, collected, or stored in personal files. Publications from the associations listed above offer help to those struggling with the privacy issue.

If you are uncertain about what public records are available in which states, there is help. *The Sourcebook of State Public Records*, second edition, from BRB Publications, is divided into categories of an amazing list of what is kept and made available by some states. For prospect and donor researchers, what is most useful are marriage, divorce, and birth and death records. The book is $33.00 and gives complete details about how to get the needed data from each state.

Call 1-602-838-8909 or order the book from a bookstore.

Here are two companies offering information taken from public documents. One is CDB Infotek with its *PeopleTracker* database. It is an investigative information service that includes civil and criminal court records, marriage records, and insurance information. Call 1-800-427-3747.

Another company providing access to public records is Database Technologies, Inc. with *Autotrack Plus*. Information gleaned from drivers' licenses, car or other property registration, professional licenses, and such is gathered and accessible by name. Call 1-800-279-7710 or 1-305-781-5221.

As more offices responsible for gathering public records become fully automated, it is certain that many companies will provide access to that information.

7

CompuServe: Best Commercial Service for Reference

"Research is formalized curiosity. It is poking and prying with a purpose."

Anonymous

Several years ago, in order to get information online, you had to subscribe to one of the major database vendors, either DIALOG, DataTimes, or through direct hookup with a particular database provider. Now, much of the same information is available through CompuServe. This commercial or consumer online service, and, to a lesser degree, America Online, Prodigy, and Microsoft Network, make the most popular databases accessible on home and office computers. Those services offer easier searching techniques, often at a cheaper rate.

By October 1995, CompuServe claimed 3.54 million subscribers. Add that figure to the rather nebulous figures for those on the Internet and you come up with a large growth rate each year, with no signs of a slowdown in new online membership. Perhaps we all should have bought stock in the companies owning these online services.

As this has happened, nonprofit organizations need to consider how they gather data and determine what aspects of this "information superhighway" will work for them. Information controls decisions made every day. It separates those who have it, and those who don't. It can mean the difference in success or failure for an organization's activities, and even for its future.

You now can have access to back issues of newspapers and magazines, directories, government documents, and reference materials on all subjects as close as your computer. You can get together with others in your field, without leaving your office. Pour yourself a cup of coffee and discuss a problem of your choice with colleagues. (More on e-mail and listservs in Chapters 10 and 11.)

Online research can be wonderful or frustrating—or both. Simultaneously. It takes some skill, developed with practice, using the trial-and-error method. There is no such thing as a perfect way to search. Each search is different. Depending on what databases you use, you may get different results, at far different costs. Often exactly the same databases are available through different vendors; some easier to use, and some more difficult. The online cost per minute may vary, depending on the vendor.

In this chapter, we will consider the reference values of commercial services, telling which contains the most useful information, first for research, and then for networking. (Forget, for now, the Internet, that big online system in the sky, that is much mentioned, but little understood by many. That is a whole other story. We'll get to that in Chapter 9.)

Of the three main commercial services, each has its strengths and weaknesses. Prodigy seems more consumer oriented, with information geared to the home or family user. CompuServe started out in much the same manner but has grown to be a good source for business and professional users because of its many databases. America Online and Microsoft Network offer some useful features. I'll discuss each separately, telling what's available on each and how to get it.

COMPUSERVE

Let's start with this because we're talking about research, not fun and games. CompuServe offers online some of the same

CompuServe: Best Commercial Service for Reference

professional reference resources you have used in print format. Perhaps you thought they were available only through direct online routes. As of September 10, 1995, CompuServe charges $9.95 per month for five hours of access to virtually all of CompuServe's services. Beyond those five hours, the charge is $2.95 per hour, down from the previous $4.80 per hour, plus database fees, if applicable.

When you venture into Premium Services, you don't pay additional for connect time unless you've used your five-hour allotment that month. You pay the charge for the database used, as you do with all online services. You will be notified when there are fees for the service you are using.

As with all online services, the minutes tick away very quickly, and downloading charges can add up. Charges are billed to your credit card, but you can get CompuServe billing information online at any time. To get charges to your account, type GO BILLING. You can print it out or choose the Mail Hardcopy option for a small fee. The billing statement shows what services were used, at what cost.

You may wish to use your home computer for office research, especially to take advantage of off-hour rates. With the itemized bill, it is simple to bill the office for research done at home. Or type GO FEEDBACK to open a business account with your password so, once approved, all account activity is billed monthly to the office.

This chapter will tell why you might want to consider joining CompuServe, and what's on it for you and your office. Although you need only communication software and a modem, it is much easier to use CompuServe with its own software, called CompuServe Information Manager (CIM), in DOS, Macintosh, or Windows versions. Free introductory membership is available, with software, by calling 1-800-524-3388.

Sometimes CompuServe software is "bundled" with new computer hardware. To sign on, all you have to do is hit a few keys or do a few clicks of your mouse. With CIM you can move within the system three ways: by selecting from a pull-down Favorite Places menu, click on an icon representing where you want to go, or click on a GO icon and type in your destination. With CIM it is easy to save an online session to disk and read it when the meter is not ticking.

Here are examples of resources from CompuServe. They cost nothing beyond the monthly fee, if the five hours per month have not been used. First, a couple general items, of use to everyone on occasion, *Grolier's Academic American Encyclopedia* is here (type GO GROLIERS to find it). Who doesn't need an encyclopedia now and then? It includes more than 10 million words in 33,000 articles. It doesn't have the pictures, or the graphics, but it's quick—and takes up no additional space in your office, as a set of encyclopedia does.

The same with a good dictionary. The *American Heritage Dictionary* (type GO DICTIONARY) includes phrases, people, and place locations.

Most word processing software includes both spell a checker and a thesaurus, so the office dictionary may be growing dusty. Having the dictionary online is still useful—like when you can't spell the word enough to be recognized by your software system. If you can type in about five characters, this online dictionary does the rest.

Hoover's Company Database is part of basic (no additional charge) services. It gives company profiles with a brief synopsis of the company, including CEO and company location. As an identification tool, it may give all that is needed for a quick business search in many nonprofit offices.

Many services on CompuServe are intended for the home audience but are useful elsewhere. *Consumer Reports* is there. It can help with purchases for an office or organization, without going to the library and paging through old issues of the magazine. It's easy to use and up to date. The same can be said for the old reliable *Peterson's College Database,* used by high school students and others seeking which of the 3,400 accredited or approved colleges to attend. In the nonprofit office, knowing the location and address of those colleges is often useful.

HEALTHNET is a service with information on diseases, symptoms, and pharmaceutical products. *Health Database Plus,* a premium service, gives more detailed information with an index to health-related articles. Who, after returning from a hurried and somewhat frustrating doctor's visit, hasn't wished for more information on the diagnosis or prescribed medication. A quick check here may answer those questions.

Both *Information Please Business Almanac* and *Information Please General Almanac* are on CompuServe, at no additional charge.

The American Airlines's reservation system, known as Eaasy Sabre, is on CompuServe (type GO EAASY SABRE). With this service, you can find flight and pricing information for your airline travel.

Premium research services are offered free of connect charges, within the five-hour option, but surcharges continue to apply for most products. This makes *DISCLOSURE II,* described below, an appealing choice for stock ownership records. *NEIGHBOR* gives an inexpensive way to get a demographic sketch of each ZIP code.

Reference services, for which there are charges, still offer a lot for your money, right there at your own computer. No longer must you trudge off to the library or sign up with a database vendor such as DIALOG.

Here's what is available with CompuServe's reference databases. All carry clearly marked fees.

KNOWLEDGE INDEX

Let's assume we all want to save money. With that in mind, this section begins with a discussion of Knowledge Index.

Chapter 5 mentioned the databases most used by staffs of nonprofit organizations with a direct DIALOG account. Despite how useful those databases are, many somewhat reluctant online searchers have failed to take the plunge and sign up with DIALOG.

In 1993 going online became easier. DIALOG, realizing there were millions of consumers connected to CompuServe needing information, decided to move their Knowledge Index service (previously available only from DIALOG) to CompuServe. Over 100 of those most-used databases are there. With that switch, DIALOG picked up many nonprofessional searchers as well as cost-conscious professional searchers. Subscribers to CompuServe can pay additional online charges to access vast amounts of information.

On Knowledge Index, time restrictions apply. The service is for those who can hang around the office after 6 p.m. (your local time) or come in before 5 a.m. Not a pleasant idea, to be sure. Better yet, it is available on weekends, between 6 p.m. Friday and 5 a.m. Monday. Knowledge Index is a good reason to use your home computer, equipped with a modem and online access to CompuServe, for office research.

CompuServe subscribers using Knowledge Index can receive many of the same databases as those using DIALOG — but at a much better price. The average Knowledge Index database online charge is $24 per hour. That's about 50 percent to 80 percent less than the regular hourly online search rate on DIALOG. Once you learn how the system works, you can do many searches for as little as $10.

Here is a list, with access codes, of databases from DIALOG on CompuServe's Knowledge Index. For more on each database, see Chapter 5. With Knowledge Index, databases are divided into categories, indicated by the first three or four letters of the group, followed by an identifying number.

"For a low one-time membership fee of $8.95 a month, you can use our most popular services... ."

CompuServe advertisement

Books

BOOK1 - *BOOKS IN PRINT*

Business and Corporate Information and News

BUS11 - *ABI/INFORM*
BUS12 - *TRADE AND INDUSTRY INDEX*
BUS15 - *BUSINESSWIRE*
BUS16 - PR *NEWSWIRE*
CORP1 - *STANDARD & POOR'S NEWS*
CORP3 - *STANDARD & POOR'S CORPORATE DESCRIPTIONS*
CORP5 - *STANDARD & POOR'S REGISTER — BIOGRAPHICAL*
LEGA1 - *LEGAL RESOURCE INDEX*

Magazines

MAGA1 - *MAGAZINE INDEX*

News

NEWS2 - *NATIONAL NEWSPAPER INDEX*

Indexes to the *Wall Street Journal,* from 1979
New York Times, from 1979
Christian Science Monitor, from 1979
Los Angeles Times, from 1982
Washington Post, from 1982
(Some indexing from other newspapers.)

The following files include full text of print newspapers from the date given to the present.

NEWS16 - *AKRON BEACON JOURNAL,* from 1989
NEWS17 - *ARIZONA REPUBLIC/PHOENIX GAZETTE,* from 1988
NEWS18 - *ATLANTA JOURNAL/ATLANTA CONSTITUTION,* from 1989
NEWS19 - *BALTIMORE SUN,* from 1989
NEWS13 - *BOSTON GLOBE,* from 1980
NEWS20 - *CHARLOTTE OBSERVER,* from 1989

NEWS12 - *CHICAGO TRIBUNE*, from 1988

NEWS21 - *CHRISTIAN SCIENCE MONITOR*, from 1989

NEWS22 - *COLUMBUS DISPATCH*, from 1988

NEWS23 - *DAILY NEWS OF LOS ANGELES*, from 1989

NEWS24 - *DETROIT FREE PRESS*, from 1987

NEWS25 - *HOUSTON POST*, from 1988

NEWS10 - *LOS ANGELES TIMES*, from 1985

NEWS26 - *MIAMI HERALD*, from 1983

NEWS15 - *NEWSDAY AND NEW YORK NEWSDAY*, from 1987 (*New York Newsday* ceased publication July 16, 1995; *Newsday* continues)

NEWS27 - *OREGONIAN* (Portland), from 1989

NEWS28 - *ORLANDO SENTINEL*, from 1988

NEWS29 - *PALM BEACH POST*, from 1989

NEWS9 - *PHILADELPHIA INQUIRER*, from 1983

NEWS39 - *PITTSBURGH PRESS*, from 1989

NEWS30 - *RICHMOND NEWS LEADER/RICHMOND TIMES DISPATCH*, from 1989

NEWS31 - *ROCKY MOUNTAIN NEWS*, from 1989

NEWS32 - *SACRAMENTO BEE*, from 1988

NEWS34 - *ST. LOUIS POST-DISPATCH*, from 1988

NEWS35 - *ST. PAUL PIONEER PRESS*, from 1988

NEWS14 - *SAN FRANCISCO*, from 1988

NEWS11 - *SAN JOSE MERCURY NEWS*, from 1985

NEWS33 - *SEATTLE TIMES*, from 1989

NEWS36 - *SUN-SENTINEL* (Fort Lauderdale), from 1988

NEWS37 - *TIMES-PICAYUNE* (New Orleans), from 1989

NEWS6 - *USA TODAY*, from 1988

NEWS8 - *WASHINGTON POST ONLINE*, from 1983

NEWS38 - *WASHINGTON TIMES*, from 1989

Full-text articles from a number of international newspapers are offered in searchable databases on CompuServe.

Examples are the *Jerusalem Post* (GO JERUSALEM), *Le Monde* from France (GO LEMONDE), *Süddeutsche Zeitung* from Germany (GO SUEDDEUT), and a variety of British papers (GO UKPAPERS) including *The Financial Times, The Guardian,* and *The Times* and *Sunday Times.*

For help in finding and using CompuServe for periodical research, see *CompuServe Companion: Finding Newspapers and Magazines Online,* a directory from BiblioData. Call 1-617-444-1154.

Having the citation to a newspaper or magazine article does little good unless you can get the article. Knowledge Index has Article Express (AEI), a document delivery system so the text of your research can be sent by postal mail, express mail or via FAX. (Type GO KI for more details.)

Reference

REFR1 - QUOTATIONS DATABASE
REFR2 - MARQUIS WHO'S WHO
REFR4 - MAGILL'S SURVEY OF CINEMA

(Okay. Admit it. You'd like to check out reviews for the neighborhood movie before you leave the office. Go ahead. Here are reviews for 1,800 notable films. Want to go straight home? Then, check what's on cable tonight and read the reviews first.)

REFR6 - CONSUMER REPORTS, from 1982
REFR8 - PUBLIC OPINION ONLINE, from 1960

Religion

RELI1 - BIBLE (KING JAMES VERSION)

Miscellaneous

Many health and human service nonprofit providers will find databases that relate to their areas. Here are some examples.

MEDI17 - AIDSLINE
MEDI10 - CANCERLIT

MED11 & 2 - MEDLINE. MEDLINE has a subdirectory called MELVYL (under DIRLINE) for physician directories.

MED111 - HEALTH PLANNING AND ADMINISTRATION

SOCS1 - SOCIOLOGICAL ABSTRACTS

OTHER COMPUSERVE PREMIUM SERVICES

Besides the bargain information on Knowledge Index, here are selected categories found to be useful to nonprofit organizations and prospect researchers. First, for those doing company research.

"I put in for reincarnation as a development officer, but they said if you don't know computers, forget it."

Business Information

Many databases found here are old reliables also available through DIALOG. For a sketch of each file, see Chapter 5. Charges range from $5 to $25 for each downloaded report. Be careful.

DISCLOSURE (GO DISCLOSURE). (Type the word or letters in parentheses to access the database.) This favorite of nonprofit prospect researchers, because of its information on stock ownership by insiders, is available in several formats: from DIALOG, and CD-ROM, and on CompuServe. This gives data on about 11,000 public companies, financial summaries, size, and business profiles. The beauty of getting this from CompuServe is that you buy just the bits and pieces you need (but even that can be expensive). You don't have to buy the whole expensive database, as with a CD-ROM.

Many are familiar with D&B *DUN'S MARKET IDENTI-FIERS* (GO DUNS) for quick corporate data. It's here also, called *DUN'S ELECTRONIC BUSINESS DIRECTORY*. It contains directory information on over 8.5 million businesses and professionals in the United States. Records include both public and private companies of all sizes and types. Information on each company usually includes name, address, telephone number, SIC code, number of employees, Dun's number, industry, and city population. Most of those elements are searchable fields.

A search on *DUN'S* will retrieve up to five companies for $7.50; each five additional companies cost another $7.50. (Prices keep changing to meet the competition. Check before using any of these databases.)

If you want to know the corporate "family" genealogy for large U.S. public companies, *CORPORATE AFFILIATIONS* (GO AFFILIATIONS) is the database telling what belongs to whom.

Many nonprofit organizations receive gifts of stocks. It is easy to find the current value (in your daily paper or the *Wall Street Journal*) but harder to find what the stocks cost when purchased. You can go to a library with newspapers on microfilm for the purchase date, or you can get the price for the last 12 years from *HISTORICAL STOCK/FUND PRICING* (GO SECURITIES).

Magazine Indexing

ZDNET databases from Ziff-Davis Publishing (GO ZD-NET) index, abstract, or provide full text for hundreds of periodicals. CompuServe is a gateway to this network. The four categories offered are: *BUSINESS DATABASE PLUS, COMPUTER DATABASE PLUS, COMPUTER BUYERS GUIDE, HEALTH DATABASE PLUS*, and *MAGAZINE DATABASE PLUS*. In case the name Ziff-Davis is not familiar, they are the folks who publish *PC Magazine* and other leading computer magazines. They have been on the front lines with electronic indexing and article retrieval for many years.

Articles on regional businesses, perhaps those you will most want to research, are available through *BUSINESS DATABASE PLUS* (GO BUSDB). About 500 regional, national, and international business and trade publications are indexed, with full text articles. Charges are 25 cents per minute (be cautious, that amounts to $15 per hour) plus $1.50 for each retrieved article. Prices vary for other databases.

For example, you are investigating the possibility of a corporate gift and hope a local business or industry might take up the challenge. Many, if not most, corporations give most generously to local organizations. After all, most philanthropy has some motive. We all want to be liked for our good deeds. So do corporations, in their own neighborhoods.

The scope for these magazine indexes is wide, from general to specific, and results are very useful. Pick a few possibilities and run the company names through these ZiffNet databases. See if there have been recent articles about the companies (and, you can hope, their philanthropic interests) in a regional or trade publication. The advantage to an in-depth article, compared to cold data from a service such as *DISCLOSURE*, is the human element. Who are the executives? What are their interests? Where do they live? Look for hints that your nonprofit organization may be of interest to the company.

For popular-type magazines, *MAGAZINE DATABASE PLUS* (GO MAGDB) offers full text of articles (but usually without the graphics) from over 130 publications. Perhaps you have experienced the frustration of going to a library for an specific article only to find it has been ripped out. Save the frustration. Find the needed article through indexing of this database, then download its full text.

PAPERCHASE (GO PAPERCHASE) gives access to *MEDLINE,* the National Library of Medicine's database of references to biomedical literature. Included are over 7 million references from 4,000 journals dating back to January 1966. To have that available on your home or office computer is quite amazing.

Newspaper Archives

As part of CompuServe's premium services, a useful archive provides access to full text (but not advertising or classified ads) for over 50 United States and United Kingdom newspapers. Articles from the late 1980s to the present are available for most newspapers. You can search by topic of interest and for a specified date range. It costs around $1.50 to view or download each article. (GO NEWSARCHIVE)

Phone Directories

Then there is *PHONE*FILE* (GO PHONEFILE). Get, as if by magic, the telephone numbers and addresses of about 80 million U.S. households. Not bad! Find your high school sweetheart. Find your stray relatives before that family reunion. Best of all, find your lost donors. Especially those major donors who have moved away but still have, you hope, your best interests at heart. Maybe they are not ignoring you. Perhaps they really didn't get your last gift solicitation letter.

Give *PHONE*FILE* a try, but don't be surprised if what you find is out of date. It's 25 cents per minute. You must have the name, plus state of residence, for it to be useful. Otherwise, with a promised 80 million residences, you will get a lot of persons with the same name.

If you are looking for a business in an out-of-state city, try *BIZ*FILE* (GO BIZFILE). It's a directory of 11 million U.S. and Canadian businesses obtained from phone books, annual reports, major business newspapers, and millions of phone calls to verify the accuracy of the data.

Consider this scenario. You're flying to a distant city to give a presentation that includes many handouts. You don't want to lug all that paper along on the plane. Use this directory to find a copy company near your hotel. Send one copy of the handout to them with instructions for reproduction. The printed papers are ready for you to pick up when you arrive in the city.

Demographic Data

Nonprofit organizations, as well as businesses, often need demographic data. Demographics is the statistical study of human populations. It can give that competitive edge when used correctly.

In describing its demographic databases in *CompuServe Magazine* (October 1994) the author described how several nonprofits used population data. For example, by determining growing and declining areas, one group determined the best sites for new churches. An organization offering low-cost loans to qualified first-time home buyers determined which neighborhoods to canvass. A health care nonprofit employee used these databases in a pilot project. The employee wanted to find needy children with English as a second language for an immunization effort.

Whatever your need, targeted marketing and fund raising requires that you know where to find those most appropriate for your solicitation.

CENDATA (GO CENDATA) is from the U.S. Census Bureau and tells housing starts, population, education, marital status, and economic information for the whole country, but available by state and county.

SUPERSITE (GO SUPERSITE) is from CACI, Inc. It allows you to narrow your search to a specific ZIP code. Reports include income, housing, racial breakdown, and education, with projection into the future. Just for kicks, check out your own ZIP code (if you are willing to pay from $25 to $45 to find out what you may already know) and see if the official version of your neighborhood fits your own image.

NEIGHBORHOOD DEMOGRAPHIC REPORTS (GO NEIGHBOR) from CACI, Inc., have four reports by ZIP code: Demographics, Civic/Public Activity, Gift Idea, and Sports/Leisure Activity. These reports cost $10 each. The CACI reports require an 80-column printer to print after downloading.

Those are some of the CompuServe databases used by nonprofit organization for company and individual prospect research. I may have missed just the one you like the most. When you subscribe to CompuServe, you will get their "New Member Guide" telling how to get started. It lists what reference databases are available and gives pricing details.

As you see, you have choices about where to get the information you need. Once you dive in, you may wish to swim around with several vendors to find the one most suited to your taste.

COMPUTRACE on CompuServe provides information from three files with information from a variety of sources. Each may have benefit for nonprofit searchers.

The Living Individuals File includes over 140 million individuals nationwide whose names appear in telephone white page directories, publishers' mailing lists (you know the ones—those that say you have just won $11 million dollars!), mail forwarding information, real estate files, and registered voter files. They give name verification and last reported address.

The Deceased Individuals File contains over 40 million individuals whose death occurred after 1928. Individuals are included if a death claim is filed by the person's spouse or dependent and the person is eligible to receive a lump-sum death payment from the Social Security Administration. It gives name verification, last reported residence, year of birth, partial social security number, date of death, and ZIP code of person who received the lump sum benefit.

The Corporations/Limited Partnerships File includes over 15 million active and inactive U.S. business names from 39 states and the District of Columbia. It tells the name, business type, status, and key contact. Information is from the Secretary of State offices in the available states.

This information from public and other records is made available from CDB Infotek, which limits the number of users at any one time so response time is not compromised. This may make it difficult to access the system. It costs 25 cents a minute, $15 per hour, in addition to any CompuServe connect time charges if you are beyond the monthly allotment.

NEED SOME HELP?

What? You are still a bit worried about doing online research? There is another choice. It may be just what you need because it offers SOS service for the timid. (Being timid amid all these choices is not a fault. It is reality, and if you don't feel a bit overwhelmed, you're unusual.) SOS help is part of IQUEST.

IQUEST (IQUEST) is a front-end or gateway service to over 800 databases from many vendors, including DIALOG, NewsNet, DataStar, and H.W. Wilson Company. IQUEST is from Telebase Systems and available on CompuServe. During earlier days of online searching, the company offered another gateway called EASYNET. This service was for the faint of heart who wished for an online human who helped with database searches, at a flat fee per search. That's still the concept, and it is now on CompuServe.

IQUEST offers two ways to retrieve information:

 • IQUEST-I guides you through a series of menus to determine which database is right for your search.

 • IQUEST-II allows you to go directly to a specified database, if you know which you want.

IQUEST provides access to multidatabase SmartSCANs so you can scan a group of databases to find those most appropriate. As with other database vendors, IQUEST offers access to the three types of databases: reference or bibliographic, abstract, and full text.

Best of all, an online human is there. Just type SOS during an IQUEST search when you need help. An "expert online research specialist" (perhaps a real-live librarian) appears in the nick of time to assist you.

IQUEST lowered its prices in early 1995, by 30 percent, according to CompuServe. Some searches can be as low as $1 or $2, with each database carrying individual charges, plus connect-time charges, depending on the need for abstracts or full text. In a full-text database, up to 15 titles are selected, plus one full-text article, from the 15. Reprinting abstracts costs $3 each and additional "hits" cost extra.

SmartSCANs cost around $5 each. If you get no hits, it still costs $1. A running total of your IQUEST session charges is displayed at each menu. To get specific pricing information for each database, type "DIR (then the database name)." You will get a description of the database with available options, including prices.

Document delivery, with photocopy reprints of articles, costs $18 or, for express service, $42.

IQUEST is available 24 hours a day, every day of the year. Remember, there is no advantage being an early bird or a night owl here. Costs are the same all day and night.

Be cautious. Some searches can get very expensive; others have surcharges, depending on the database used. Some have very expensive full records. (To be fair, these are the same ones that are expensive no matter where you find them.) You might want to talk to that SOS person and get some idea what your search will cost before you start.

To give an example from that much-used MARQUIS WHO'S WHO. With IQUEST it costs $16 per search. That's a good candidate to use through Knowledge Index during off hours. Or call your public library telephone reference department for a free quick search. Another tip is to use Knowledge Index for newspaper searches. They are usually pretty straightforward searches, where no expert help is needed.

Keep in mind, if the needed database is under the DIALOG or another vendor umbrella, you can probably get to it on CompuServe through IQUEST. (An exception is *LEXIS-NEXIS*.) Once you are hooked up to CompuServe, you can print out a list of what's available with a short description of each and pricing information.

Here are examples of IQUEST databases not available on DIALOG and thus not on Knowledge Index either. All have potential use to nonprofits researchers. The database vendor is in parentheses.

AGELINE

Contains references to and abstracts of materials on aging and the aged. (CD PLUS Technologies) $9 per search

AIDS DATABASE

Includes critically selected articles on all aspects of AIDS and AIDS-related research. (DataStar) $14 per search

BIOGRAPHY INDEX

This database corresponds to the useful printed *Biography Index* from H.W. Wilson Company. It indexes books, journals, book reviews, bibliographies, and interviews. (H.W. Wilson Company) $9 per search

CHURCHNEWS INTERNATIONAL

News from churches and religious agencies associated with the National and World Council of Churches. It addresses such issues as peace, ethnicity, corporate responsibility, human rights, women's concerns, etc. (NewsNet, Inc.) $9 per search

CORPORATE GIVING WATCH

This tracks new trends in corporate philanthropy. It includes monthly profiles on major corporate giving programs with full text of the newsletter. (NewsNet, Inc.) $9 per search

CUADRA DIRECTORY OF ONLINE DATABASES

It contains a directory of publicly accessible online databases worldwide. It records database type, subject, language, and time span, with names and addresses of database producer and online services. (DataStar) $11 per search

EDUCATION DAILY

This full-text newsletter contains current reports on events for education officials from the Department of Education, Congress, and the courts concerning the latest on civil rights, vocational training and research. (NewsNet, Inc.) $9 per search

EDUCATION INDEX

References from this database cover all aspects of education from English-language periodicals. (H.W. Wilson Company) $9 per search

FEDERAL GRANTS AND CONTRACTS WEEKLY

Covers U.S. federal government grants in research, training, and services. Includes news and analysis and updates on new legislation, publications, and foundations. (NewsNet, Inc.) $9

FOUNDATION GIVING WATCH

This full text of the newsletter provides giving policies, contract information, and lists of recent grants for leading private philanthropic institutions. Includes new funding opportunities and trends in foundation philanthropy. (NewsNet, Inc.) $9 per search

HEALTH & HOSPITALS NEWSLETTERS

Gives full text of a collection of newsletters covering all aspects of health and hospitals. (NewsNet, Inc.) $9 per search

HEALTH GRANTS AND CONTRACTS WEEKLY

Provides coverage of health-related federal grants and contracts. Includes updates on related legislation and news about key funding agencies. Full text. (NewsNet, Inc.) $9 per search

HEALTH NEWS DAILY

Reports on world health industry developments. It focuses on industry and trade professional associations and all aspects of health care. (NewsNet, Inc.) $9 per search

INDEX TO LEGAL PERIODICALS

This covers all aspects of jurisprudence. Emphasizes copyright and patent law, tax law, international law, malpractice statutes, case notes, and book reviews. (H.W. Wilson Company) $9 per search

INTERNATIONAL STOCKS DATABASE

Provides full text of business information on companies publicly traded on many exchanges worldwide. (News-Net, Inc.) $9 per search

MEDLINE

Indexes articles from medical journals published worldwide. Corresponds to *Index Medicus*. (CD PLUS Technologies) $9 per search

NEW ENGLAND JOURNAL OF MEDICINE

Full text clinical and scientific articles in the field of medicine from this top medical journal. (CD PLUS Technologies) $9 per search

PAIS INTERNATIONAL

Indexes articles, books, and government documents on public policy worldwide. Includes economics, business, political, and social sciences. (DataStar) $11 per search

READERS' GUIDE ABSTRACTS

Covers abstracts to articles going back to 1983 from popular magazines. Corresponds to the printed *Readers' Guide to Periodical Literature*. (H.W. Wilson Company) $9 per search

Okay. If you can't find a useful database from all those choices, you may not be trying. It is your choice whether you want to do online searching, but if you don't you are missing a world of information at your fingertips.

Here's an example of useful corporate research with *FORTUNE* (GO FORTUNE) on CompuServe. With it you can download the Fortune 500, the premier listing of top industrial companies in the United States, or the Service 500 for banks, insurance, retail, and utilities companies. There is even a Most Admired Corporations list, based on a survey of key decision makers who rated the companies according to a number of criteria.

Forbes Magazine has a presence on CompuServe also. In a 1991 speech, Malcolm "Steve" Forbes Jr. hailed the high-tech revolution and five years later his Capitalist Tool, as his magazine is called, is now cyber-savvy and online. Beginning in November 1995, CompuServe shows the current issue. Later, back issues will be accessible with menu commands. Did you miss the Forbes' list of the 400 richest Americans? Don't despair. It's here, in a Forbes List section (GO FORBES). Once into the list area, you can read, download, or print information on your favorite hoped-for donor. Better than the print version, the online edition allows users to search by last name, state, or minimum net worth.

Forbes' readers love lists, it seems. The magazine has capitalized on this thirst for years, offering many annual rankings of the largest public and private companies. Other lists and rankings of corporations will be added as published.

COMPUSERVE CLIPPING SERVICE

One of the features of CompuServe's Executive News Service, for an extra fee, is an electronic "clipping service." Check with CompuServe to set up an account for this service. Then, you tell the service what to watch for, in a selected group of newspapers or databases, and it will scan up to five sources daily for stories that match a search profile you have created.

You create a folder into which the chosen articles will be put and specify a name, a company, or any combination of keywords for which the scan is to search. Spend some time planning what words or names to use. If your choice is too narrow, you may miss the information; if too broad, you will be snowed under with too many captured articles. There is a limit of 500 stories per folder, and a folder can fill up quickly.

You will need to set limits to your search, plus set an expiration date, and say how many day's worth of stories will be held in your folder. Help is available online. Use it, and ask for the price before you get carried away with this service.

FORUMS ON COMPUSERVE

One much-used feature of commercial online services is the variety of special-interest forums for members. There, members can download documents, chat with like-minded persons, look for marketing features, and read notices.

A few forums are listed here.

Catholics Online (GO CATHOLIC) is a forum for Roman Catholics on CompuServe. Created summer 1995, it includes files on subjects such as church and papal history, the Bible, abortion issues, religious education, and religious graphics. Members can post and read messages online.

NonProfit Forum, begun fall 1995, is an add-on forum, available for $15 extra each month. It offers information on most aspects of nonprofit management, including fund raising. Documents are available for downloading from its library of resources, and career opportunities are posted. There's even a "chat" area called "The Among Friends Cafe" where you can communicate with others. Bring your own coffee. For details, GO NONPROFIT or e-mail to 75162.3366 @CompuServe.com.

Genealogy Forum (GO ROOTS) helps you research your own, or prospective donor's, family tree. Many members on this forum have had extensive experience researching family histories and pass along tips and shortcuts.

Information USA (GO US) has extensive listings of free government publications and how to get them. It tells of federal grants and research services available for individuals, organizations, and small businesses.

Issues + (GO ISSUES +) has sections for many social issues and a section for nonprofit organizations. It gives useful documents, information on publications and a place to chat about nonprofit issues.

United Way of America (GO UW) tells about the agencies and charities funded by United Way. It shows how to volunteer or how to get help through those organizations, in the old fashioned way—by telephone.

There are more forums on CompuServe, perhaps some meeting exactly your career and individual interests. There are even country-specific forums offering a variety of information on many areas of the world.

Once subscribed to CompuServe, the *CompuServe Magazine* will keep you informed as services and forums are added. Each monthly issue gives very useful tips for making the best use of the service.

INTERNET ACCESS

CompuServe provides direct access to the Internet with a system called Mosaic. Time spent reading WWW and Gopher sites count toward the monthly allotment.

8

America Online and Commercial Services: Plus Some Networks

*"The principle that information is good lies
at the heart of representative democracy."*

Vice President Al Gore

As Knight-Ridder Information DIALOG is the best direct-access database vendor for nonprofit research, CompuServe is the most useful commercial online service for those researchers. In fact, many, if not most, of the databases one needs from DIALOG are available through CompuServe. It's often a toss-up which is the most economical way to search—directly from DIALOG or via CompuServe, using Knowledge Index or other gateway techniques.

If you are connected to a commercial service and use it, either at home or in the office, for e-mail or to access forums and support groups, you can find some very useful databases scattered throughout these services. As with CompuServe, on these online services, you get free time to play around in the service before attempting any reference database for which a charge is levied. Play in the wading pool before diving into the big pool.

All of these services are considered consumer online services, meaning they mostly are used in homes. Most do, in fact, offer consumer information. Because some include selective databases of interest, or of use, to those in nonprofit organization, they are included here.

All charge basic rates of about $10 per month, so require no large investment to experiment. In fact, most offer your first month free.

AMERICA ONLINE

Aggressive marketing by America Online has made it the fastest growing online service. By October 1995, it had signed up 3.8 million subscribers, with about 5,600 new members signing up each day.

If you have bought a computer in the past few years you may have received software to hook up with AOL bundled with your purchase or in the mail soon after your purchase. The free software serves as a buffer to connect you to the AOL host computer. It contains graphic elements, icons, and help to make your online trip easy. To get into the service you want, either click on the icon, or enter a keyword.

Its ease of use notwithstanding, does AOL include any reference resources you want or need? That ever-present encyclopedia is there, but this time it's *Compton's Living Encyclopedia*. It's not as complete as the *Grolier's Electronic Encyclopedia* found elsewhere. But you want more than an encyclopedia.

Anything vaguely called reference is included in the Learning & Reference section. Sometimes this category is a bit misleading. The listing for "Library of Congress Online" offers some sample graphics and text files from various exhibits at the Library but, unfortunately, offers no access to that vast reference center.

PERIODICAL ACCESS WITH AMERICA ONLINE

The Main Menu on America Online offers a category called Newsstand. Click on it to see what newspapers and magazines are available, then click the wanted title. Many weekly and monthly magazines are here. *Time Magazine* is here. You can read it online before it hits your mailbox.

You might want to consider dropping subscriptions to those magazines you just don't have time to read. On AOL you can scan the magazine's table of content for articles that interest you. Zap the actual articles into a file on your hard disk to read at your leisure or come back to them at a later time. (Be careful. In some cases, only the latest edition is here. Other publications provide database access to past issues.)

THE NEW YORK TIMES

America Online includes the daily *New York Times* (called *@times*). Although it has no archival access, it is a good, and inexpensive, way to get that paper's news, columns, and editorials if you already belong to AOL. The day's news is organized into six categories: Page One, International, National/ Metro, Business, Sports, and Arts. News articles appear about 11:30 p.m. the evening before the daily edition and remain posted for two days. Classified ads from the *Sunday Times* remain posted for one week.

Perhaps you remember a *Times* article you read on AOL. How do you find it later? For those specific articles from back issues, you are advised to visit a library with the *New York Times Index* and the newspaper on either CD-ROM or microfilm. Articles from back issues can be found with direct access to *LEXIS/NEXIS*. Or, you can call NEXIS Express (1-800-843-6476) for a search for *Times* articles. It will send full-text printouts charged to your major credit card.

THE CHICAGO TRIBUNE

Those in the Midwest may be more interested in a Chicago paper. AOL offers *Chicago Online,* a gateway to the *Tribune Archives* database containing all the articles published in the daily and *Sunday Chicago Tribune* since 1985. You can search for, and then print out, the actual article.

This is a premium service with prime-time (Monday to Friday, 6 a.m. to 6 p.m. Central Time) at $1.25 per minute of access time. All other time is non-prime-time at 15 cents per minute. Regular AOL connect charges apply. As with all online full-text searching, plan your search very carefully before you click in.

ARIZONA REPUBLIC/PHOENIX GAZETTE

Watch for AOL access to this Phoenix newspaper. So far, clicking on its title gives only interesting facts about the city and state taken from the paper. Keyword and subject search capacity is promised soon—perhaps by the time you read this.

SAN JOSE MERCURY NEWS

This home town paper of the Silicon Valley in California is available on AOL as *Mercury Center*. It offers two ways to search for information: the News Library and Text Search. The first gives access to articles back to July 1985. Text Search is more limited, using keywords to search today's paper and selected articles that were electronically posted into *Mercury Center* by category.

One interesting and potentially useful feature of America Online is NewsHound (keyword: newshound.) The *Mercury Center* Newshound seems named after the faithful mutt who goes to the front step to fetch the daily paper. This clipping service, which costs $4.95 per month, allows you to set up a profile of terms (perhaps your corporate donors or wealthy prospects) you want checked. The Hound then hourly scans the *San Jose Mercury News* and various wire services. It delivers relevant articles to your e-mailbox as it is collected. *Mercury Center,* an online service of the *San Jose Mercury News,* is owned by Knight-Ridder.

"Your Optional 500-Sheet Paper Tray Assembly is covered under your printer's one-year warranty or 90 days, whichever is longer."

HP LaserJet 4 Manual (PC Magazine, August 1994

Where the Information Is

In the *Mercury Center*'s News Library you can search back issues of 16 other newspapers. That's useful, especially if you live in a distant part of the country and need just an occasional obituary or other newspaper search. It is a fee-based service, at 15 cents per minute off-peak and 80 cents per minute during peak times, weekdays between 6 a.m. to 6 p.m., Pacific Time, charged on your America Online bill.

These papers are now available:
Akron (Ohio) *Beacon Journal* - from 1985
The Boston Globe - from 1980
The Charlotte (North Carolina) *Observer* - from 1985
The State (Columbia, South Carolina) - from 1987
The News Sentinel (Fort Worth, Indiana) - from 1990
Post-Tribune (Gary, Indiana) - from 1987
Lexington (Kentucky) *Herald-Leader* - from 1983
(Memphis, Tennessee) *Commercial Appeal* - from 1990
Press-Telegraph (Long Beach, California) - from 1990
Daily News (Los Angeles, California) - from 1985
The Miami Herald - from 1983
The Philadelphia Inquirer - from 1981
Philadelphia Daily News - from 1978
Denver's Rocky Mountain News - from 1989
San Jose Mercury News - from 1985
St. Paul (Minnesota) *Pioneer Press* - from 1988
The Wichita (Kansas) *Eagle* - from 1984

BUSINESS INFORMATION

Business directories on AOL give some information. *Hoover's Business Resources* (keyword: hoover) gives quick identification of companies, with location and top executive information for about 8,000 companies worldwide. The subjects covered include business history, market data, competition, and proucts produced. A Business Rankings section grades companies and lists them in special categories, like those most socially responsible.

Stock reports are here and updated hourly. They are easily available by stock symbol. What, you don't know the symbol?

Click into the Personal Finance section, then go to Quotes and Portfolios. Click Lookup Symbol, then follow the alphabetical list path to discover the stock symbol. Then, you're on your way.

As a consumer commercial service, it is no surprise that many sections of AOL deal with personal finance. That does not mean you will not find useful data here for your nonprofit office. An inexpensive corporate search done on AOL may get you started and, at least, identify a corporate prospect or donor.

Once identified, you can get many SEC filings on AOL through *EdgarPlus Database* (keyword: edgar). 10-Ks (annual reports) and 10-Qs (quarterly reports) are here and easily found. After using the keyword, pick the needed files provided by Disclosure, Inc. Each year, more and more public companies have been electronically filing their required reports. By 1996 all companies must file that way.

TRAVEL

If you want to act as your own agent for airline tickets, America Online offers access to America Airlines' reservation system, known as *Eaasy Sabre* (keyword: eaasy). You can find the best route, at the best price, then connect to Express Net (keyword: expressnet). That is a service from American Express that lets their card holders make airline reservations directly, bypassing a travel agent. *Eaasy Sabre* is on CompuServe and Prodigy also.

Many travel forums and special areas, arranged by country and city, provide tourist information so you can plan your journey before you leave home.

TAXES

When April 15 comes around and you realize you are missing a crucial tax form, AOL can save the day. *The Tax Forum* (keyword: tax) has a wide collection of federal tax forms that you can download, with a document format viewer. As the tax-due date gets closer, you can find helpful tax tips online.

FORUMS AND SPECIAL AREAS

Perhaps the most useful and interesting parts of America Online are its forums and special-interest groups. Many are societies and associations related to specific diseases that offer forums and "chat rooms." Examples are the National Multiple Sclerosis Society (NMSS) and the United Cerebral Palsy Association (UCPA).

Others, such as *LatinoNet,* offer information and discussion for that market, both in this country and in Latin America. LatinoNet has information on nonprofit organizations and foundations that fund Latino organizations. It encourages persons from the Latino community to become computer literate.

An example of a nonprofit organization's use of America Online is the section devoted to The Nature Conservancy.

"This is Teach a Man to Fish Foundation. How may I direct your call?"

Besides some current information about nature walks and bird watching, there is sufficient information for a good picture of the organization. Online users can click on ways to support The Nature Conservancy, how to begin or renew membership, how to "Adopt-An-Acre" or "Adopt-A-Bison" (from afar, one hopes), or find ways to give to that organization.

It tells how to contact The Nature Conservancy to volunteer or contribute. There is even a marketplace area, with T-shirts and other logo items for sale. What better way to get facts about your organization known to the potential millions of America Online members? AOL users use the keyword "nature" to find The Nature Conservancy section.

In 1995 AOL began a *Nonprofit Professional Network* (keyword: access.point) to serve both nonprofit personnel and volunteers. It promises to be a cross between a professional conference and a resource library of articles that can be downloaded, right there at your own desk. It's a starting place for organizations wishing to network through AOL's Information Technology Consulting. When the service began, nonprofit organizations with national constituencies were solicited to become part of the service. Later, smaller groups were asked to become involved.

On AOL, there is an emphasis on citizen involvement in what's going on in Washington, with one forum on the White House, with copies of press releases and transcripts available to subscribers. Access to selected National Public Radio and Television programs are available.

America Online offers good Internet World Wide Web access with fairly easy instructions for its use. As getting on "the Net" is now much sought-after, this is one route.

America Online costs $9.95 per month, which includes five hours online. Additional time is $2.95 per hour. (As with other commercial online services, prices are subject to change.)

In summary, for access to a wide variety of experiences, try America Online. but for serious research, go CompuServe.

Call America Online at 1-800-827-6364 or 1-703-448-8700.

PRODIGY

Prodigy is the third largest consumer online service with 1.72 million members. (CompuServe had 3.54 million members in October 1995.) Prodigy fits into the consumer online service category—no surprise because it is jointly owned by Sears and IBM. It is not very useful for the serious researcher. It does include some interesting items, like *Consumer Reports,* the *Magilll's Movie Guide,* and *Zagat Restaurant Survey.* Go ahead, plan what restaurants you want to visit when you're in a distant city for the next NSFRE or ARPA conference.

Markets at a Glance on Prodigy offers a 30-day overview of companies that list their stocks on any of the stock exchanges. It carries business news and access to *PR Newswire* and *PC Financial Network.*

Another service, *Company Reports,* lets you search for company information by entering the stock symbol. If you don't know it, Prodigy gives help. Five-page reports on stock performance over the past year are available for $1.95; for an additional 50 cents, you can see the results graphed by average highs and lows, then compared to the Standard and Poor's 500.

Prodigy has the reputation of being for children, with its basic encyclopedia, useful for homework, and lots of games. For adults there are forums, here called bulletin boards.

As other services do, Prodigy offers Internet World Wide Web access. Perhaps of some interest to nonprofits was Prodigy's success as the first big commercial online service to let members "publish" their own material on the Internet's World Wide Web, by creating a Home Page. Both America Online and CompuServe followed Prodigy with the home page option.

Prodigy offers many bulletin boards for like-minded individuals, but has the controversial practice of moderating bulletin board messages and deleting curse words, hate speech (an extreme form of "flaming"), and what they consider messages inappropriate for family consumption. For some, this is a desirable feature.

Prodigy costs $9.95 a month for five hours, plus $2.95 per extra hour. Access to the Web is provided at no additional cost.

Call Prodigy at 1-800-776-3449, extension 638, or 1-914-448-8000.

MICROSOFT NETWORK

Microsoft Network debuted as part of Windows '95 from Microsoft and soon became the fourth largest commercial service with 200,000 members by October 1995. With such easy access from Windows '95, it led to some controversy with other services. They felt Microsoft Network had an unfair advantage. Whether it will offer much, or anything, for nonprofits besides e-mail and access to the Internet remains to be seen. It will probably take a while to get up to speed, but with Microsoft's millions behind it, it may be worth watching.

One feature that can be useful to nonprofit organizations is designed for business owners. It is *CCH Business Owner's Toolkit,* from a business-consulting firm specializing in assisting small businesses. It offers a handy and varied collection of advice on hiring, firing, tax law, and legislative information.

Before the end of its first year, Microsoft Network decided the future was in offering a gateway to Internet access rather than trying to compete with CompuServe or America Online with a variety of databases. This change of emphasis showed just how quickly the Internet has taken over the online world. If it is possible to surprise Bill Gates, this seems to have done it.

The standard monthly subscription for three hours is $4.95, with a $2.50 charge for additional hours. There are several frequent-user annual or monthly plans.

Call Microsoft Network at 1-800-386-5550.

GENIE

GEnie (no longer called GEnie, after its previous General Electric parent) has new management in 1996 and a new outlook on life. While never one of the major commercial online players, Genie now hopes to emerge as a major Internet provider. It is now owned by Yovell Renaissance Corporation.

It offers direct Internet access for $29 per month with no additional charges for hours spent online.

Call Genie at 1-800-638-9636 or 1-301-340-4000.

AT&T INTERCHANGE

Most commercial online services are generalists, with something for everyone. Others hope to create their own niche, with emphasis on one topic. AT&T Interchange operates like an online network, accepting third-party content providers, each offering deep information within a limited topic spectrum.

Within this network are *AT&T Business Network, ZD NET, Washington Post Digital Ink,* and *Star Tribune Online.* Although loosely connected, each carries its own monthly subscription fee.

AT&T Business Network hopes to be the service for business people to learn about running a business. It debuted in late 1995 and includes many, if not most, business databases mentioned throughout this book. It is a way to access *Standard & Poor's, Dun & Bradstreet, TRW Business Information, Dow Jones,* and others. It also offers Internet access.

Washington Post Digital Ink and *Star Tribune Online* both offer their respective newspapers' content, with back files going back several years. Both offer community information and local services for the District of Columbia and Minneapolis/ St.Paul areas, respectively. Similar service from Connecticut's *New Haven Register* is expected soon. Because these newspapers archive their articles and news stories for retrieval online, it is like having an indexed stack of thousands of daily newspapers on your desk. In fact, much better.

Call *AT&T Business Network* at 1-800-665-4492. For those in the region of the three online newspapers, contact them directly.

NEW CENTURY NETWORK

This network was in development in late 1995. It is a joint venture of several large newspaper owners (those owning more than 200 daily newspapers) to put their newspapers into the network that will enable personal computer users to call up news articles and other information from participating newspapers. The group promised the *New York Times* will be one of the first newspapers online with this network.

THE ONLINE COMMUNITY OF NETWORKS

Many networks were developed as nonprofit organizations to meet the needs for those interested in specific topics. Grassroots organizations realized they were no longer alone. Through networking with like-minded organizations, they could benefit. In the past few years, over 10,000 groups have joined networks, and more are going online each month. Nonprofit networks realize the special needs that most organizations have, then gather data to meet those concerns. With easy distribution of information online to members, groups around the country can unite around common causes.

The Benton Foundation in Washington, DC, provides leadership and tools to strengthen communications capacities of nonprofit organizations. It encourages the use of the techniques and technologies of communications to advance the democratic process. Its mission "is to gain an effective voice for social change and to shape the emerging communications environment, creating an expanded vision of the social benefits of new technologies."

One of the publications of the foundation, *Electronic Networking for Nonprofits: A Guide to Getting Started,* by Tom Sherman, describes the technical basis of networking and tells how to implement an appropriate network.

Here are examples of large networks that provide services to nonprofits or work toward some of the same objectives as other nonprofit organizations.

THE WELL

Virtual communities are somewhere between a common-interest bulletin board and a full-service commercial online system. They were formed to make online connections, both electronically and socially. One of the early ones was The

WELL (Whole Earth 'Lectronic Link). Community building remains an important part of its mission. Ideas and opinions fly back and forth on a multitude of nonprofit ideas. It has full Internet access.

For voice information, call 1-415-332-4335.

ECHO

As The WELL is thought to be a west coast community, ECHO (East Coast Hang Out) is a regional, New York City-flavored virtual community with a high proportion of women subscribers (about 40 percent). Women's Online Network was created to involve more women in political action and to provide a forum to develop strategies to improve the position of women in society. That conference of ECHO is now controlled by *Ms. Magazine*. It has a nominal subscription fee and is connected to the Internet. Call 1-212-255-3839 or send an e-mail message to info@echonyc.com.

WOMEN'S WIRE

The first online system to focus primarily on women's issues and information is Women's Worldwide Information and Resource Exchange (Women's WIRE). Realizing that only 10 to 20 percent of online users were women when it started, this service aims to attract and train more female network users by bringing women's organizations and publications to its system. Started in San Francisco in 1994, this network maintains a database on women's health, history, employment, and politics. Nonprofit organizations can post solicitation messages online. In early 1996, Women's WIRE joined CompuServe, where 17 percent of its subscribers are women. To reach Women's WIRE, type GO WOMEN while you are in CompuServe.

USENET

Most networks use a Usenet or "bulletin board on the Internet" to connect to each other. A single forum for discussion on Usenet is called a newsgroup. You can join Usenet for free, and read the postings or messages others have left. Then, if you wish to reply, you can type your message and send it to the group, as you would with e-mail. Unlike e-mail, though, postings on Usenet are public—anyone may browse and read the messages. More than 10,000 different newsgroups on every imaginable topic circulate among 80 countries. Each is read by thousands daily.

INSTITUTE FOR GLOBAL COMMUNICATIONS (IGC)

Devoted solely to environmental preservation, peace, women's issues, and human rights, the IGC network began in 1985. It supports *PeaceNet* (for disarmament and peace activists), *EcoNet* (for environmentalists), *ConflictNet* (for those hoping to resolve conflicts), and *LaborNet* (for union activists). It is concerned with bringing network communication to disadvantaged parts of the world.

In 1994, *EcoNet* and *PeaceNet* combined had a total of more than 8,000 subscribers, about 60 percent of them nonprofit groups. *ConflictNet* and *LaborNet* add another 500 to the network. Each month more organizations join to receive e-mail services, database information, and connection to the Internet. Online public conferences on environmental and human rights topics are another much-used feature. *EcoNet,* for example, has held conferences on fund raising for nonprofits, where groups can share ideas and work on joint grant proposals.

Call 1-415-442-0220 for information.

HANDSNET

Human service providers are linked in this network that started in 1986. Several people sat around a table in Cupertino, California, and started thinking of more efficient ways to share ideas. A computer network was suggested, with the hope that members would realize there were more uses for computers than word processing.

As membership in HandsNet grew, it developed partnerships with other nonprofit groups and helped them develop their own specialized sub-networks. HandsNet furnishes training, software, and technical assistance so those groups can use e-mail systems and online conferences. Online forums offer members the chance to post messages and exchange ideas.

For a packet of information call 1-408-257-4500 or e-mail to HN0012@handsnet.org.

JOIN TOGETHER COMPUTER NETWORK

An example of a subnetwork, as described in *infoActive: The Telecommunications Monthly for Nonprofits,* is Join To-gether Computer Network. It links almost 300 substance abuse coalitions to share experiences and information. Each month 400 articles and news summaries in the field are provided on-line. The network tracks legislation and provides a calendar of events. Other subnetworks are *HealthLink USA* and *Families USA.*

For information, call HandsNet at 1-408-257-4500.

CJF ONLINE

CJF is an online computer service run by the Council of Jewish Federations that links staff and board members from its many federations around the country. It helps members take advantage of the vast resources on the global Internet, and pro-vides access to it. It provides electronic forums on nonprofit topics such as planned giving and fund raising. An annual fee offers unlimited online use.

For further information, e-mail to fstrauss@cjf.noli.com or call 1-212-598-3516.

The networks mentioned above are just a few examples from the vast number of networks used by nonprofit organiza-tions. They provide e-mail and other electronic technology to improve service to the community served.

9

Internet: A Tool for the Future of Nonprofits

> *"The 'Net will soon be much more than a useful tool for nonprofits; it will be a necessity. In the future, trying to run a nonprofit without the Internet will be like trying to run one without a telephone."*
>
> Taylor Walsh
> Cap Access of Washington, D.C.

This book will not tell all there is to know about the Internet. Wouldn't it be nice if it could! It would be impossible, and would fill volumes. If you have looked for a simple Internet book at your bookstore, you will find no such thing. One thing you can be sure of is that the book will be, partly at least, out of date before you get it home. That is not just this author's cop-out; it is a reality. Among the best, and the worst, things you can say about the Internet is that it is not static.

Currently, well over 200 books are in print with the word Internet in the title. It is hard to determine which is the best one. (Perhaps that is why the "Dummies" series of books is so popular. These books speak to our insecurities. Most of them, it seems. The company has now gone to subjects beyond computers. Recent books are *Wine For Dummies* and *Sex For Dummies*.)

The Internet books, with titles declaring their simplicity, can be three inches thick—over 500 pages. This book can't and won't compete with them. It really is not necessary. Perhaps more has been written about the Internet, or the information superhighway, in the last two years than about any other subject. If you want, or need, to know more than is given here (and you might) check the bibliography at the back of this book for some ideas. Or look at any bookstore for new titles.

This book will mention what the Internet can do for you, for your nonprofit organization, and, more specifically, for development officers and prospect researchers. If you have been using the Internet for years, congratulations. You know its potential and may want to read this chapter just to see what, if anything, is missing. You'll be the first to admit that the Internet changes daily and there may be really great resources not covered here. When you find them, tell your friends. Also, the resources for finding information on the Internet discussed in the next chapters may lead others to the information you have discovered.

This chapter is for those of you who may be new to the Internet or still a bit intimidated by it. Even though you have warmed up to online searching, through DIALOG or, perhaps, CompuServe, you may still consider the Internet sort of uncharted territory.

This is also for those who have wanted to dive into the Internet, but either haven't dared or haven't been sure there was anything for them once they made the plunge. They don't know what equipment is needed, how to get hooked up, what it will cost, how to find their way around the world to which they are now connected, or whether it is worth the trouble. Those previously mentioned Internet old-timers look askance at the newcomers (even their name—newbies—is a bit demeaning), wondering why they are so intimidated by the Internet. "It's really fun and easy, isn't it?" the skilled say. "It's a bit complicated," say the novices. Both are right.

First of all, there is no user manual to the Internet. There are lots of guides. Go into any computer or bookstore and take a serious look on the shelves. The guides may cover more than you need, or want, to know. In them, there is a tendency to tell everything the author knows, just in case someone might want to know about a little-known, previously unannounced corner of the Internet. Most such guides are written for the generalist. This is for you in the nonprofit world only. Items discussed will pertain to you and your work.

The Internet has been compared to visiting New York or Paris. Both are "wondrous places full of great art and artists, stimulating coffee houses and salons, towers of commerce, screams and whispers, romantic hideaways, dangerous alleys, great libraries, chaotic traffic, rioting students, and a population that is rarely characterized as warm and friendly." (*New York Times,* April 5, 1994)

The comparison is not bad. The Internet population is larger than the equivalent of New York and Paris combined, and it is growing daily. First-time visitors or users might have a hard time finding their way around, especially if they do not understand the language or have a street map. Some say the Internet is an enormous library with no card catalog. People look around and leave.

There are two main types of Internet users: the core users and the consumer users. The first category comprises those with computers that are fully linked to the Internet and thus able to connect to other computers across the country or the world to look at files stored there. This is what has been considered the Internet since it began over 20 years ago. Those are the folks with accounts through universities, corporations, associations, the government, or scientific organizations. Many in nonprofit offices have these accounts.

It is no surprise that those core users who become authorities on the Internet and used it for prospect research and other nonprofit uses were connected to universities.

Researchers tend to be adventurous souls. With the campus computers hooked up, it was a very natural progression to see how the Internet could connect like-minded people at other institutions to talk about fund raising and prospect research online. These, like other Internet users are looking for one thing: information. Where it is, and how to find it.

Add the second category, those who in 1995 gained full access to the Internet through commercial online services such as CompuServe and America Online, and you get millions more. During the same period, many homes and offices connected to the Internet with local service providers.

The number of Internet users is growing quickly. The number with some access to the Internet is approximately doubling in size each year and has been doing so for at least the past six years. Don't be the last organization on your block to see what's on the Internet for you.

The Internet is a valuable tool in the right hands or for those who understand what it is and what it isn't. The danger, said one office manager, is its "all-you-can-eat-for-free nature." You can spend a lot of time searching for trivia everywhere.

Forever. That same manager said there can be a "giant productivity-sucking sound when users log on to the Internet." Those employees who find time to play solitaire on their computers, "just because it came already installed," may enjoy the thrill of the chase on the Internet.

HISTORY OF THE INTERNET.
WHERE DID IT COME FROM?

In 1969, the U.S. Defense Department wanted a connection between its ARPANET and various other radio and satellite networks. ARPA stands for the Advanced Research Projects Agency. ARPANET was an experimental network designed to support military research. This was heavy-duty research. The researchers needed a network that could withstand partial outages (like from nuclear bomb attacks!) and still function, through a maze of connecting computers. In case much of the country was wiped out, these folks could still communicate. I guess that is a comforting thought, but I'm not sure.

As the network developed and worked, more and more government and academic research users became addicted to this process of communicating and exchanging data. Demand for networking quickly spread. Ethernet local area networks (LANs) were developed. By about 1983 desktop workstations became available and local networking exploded. Those LANs wanted to connect beyond their university or company to a network such as the already established ARPANET. Most sites used UNIX, a popular operating software developed at the University of California at Berkeley.

One of those local networks wanting part of the action was the National Science Foundation (NSF). In the late 1980s NSF created five supercomputer centers at major universities. Scholarly researchers hooked on. At first, NSF connected to the ARPANET for communications. That attempt failed because of bureaucratic and staffing problems. The solution was to build its own network using preexisting technology—telephone lines. Regional networks allowed schools to connect to the nearest neighbor and, ultimately, to a supercomputer center. In this manner, any computer could eventually communicate with others, through its neighbors. That version became the NSFNET.

In 1987, a contract was awarded to upgrade the old network with faster telephone lines and faster computers. The Internet became not a network but a collection of networks, like the network of telephone companies throughout the world. All are separate, but can connect to others, almost anywhere in the world. Just dial the number; don't worry about the route the call takes to the person called. The Internet can also get you almost anywhere. Currently over 60 countries are connected, and the number of countries is growing each year as telephone systems become more reliable in the third world. Having country access on the Internet sounds better than it is. Access is probably limited only to a few sites in many countries.

Because the emphasis of NSF is research, it allowed access to the Internet to virtually every four-year college in the country. NSF promoted this education access by funding campus connections with the hope that students would become eager Internet users. They did. As did government and corporate employees, small business owners, nonprofit organizations, and, eventually, end users at home.

Because many of the first Internet users were students at major universities, who did not pay for its use, a myth grew that the Internet was free. It isn't. Someone pays for each connection though, perhaps, not the individual. Someone pays for the connection to the regional network, which, in turn, pays the national provider for its access. Access through an Internet

"Immediate Hire: $40,000-$50,000. Division of high-profile co. seeking a programmer analyst with 305 years UNIX experience."

Fort Collins Coloradoan (PC Magazine, August 1994

provider costs by the month, and may cost for time online. For many, the costs of the Internet are largely absorbed by their institutions and the federal government.

This explains why researchers connected to a university, whether in the science labs or development offices, were leaders who used the Internet for whatever type of research they were doing.

Many of the networks in the Internet are sponsored by federal agencies, thus they use federal dollars. As networks evolved, one requirement was that they be "in support of research or education." This provision allowed legitimate use by a wide range of users. Although, originally, commercial use of networks was prohibited, there are now commercial networks, operating on different fee structures.

What was begun for research evolved as a means of disseminating information. Thus the information superhighway phrase became part of the national vocabulary. Its potential is just beginning to be realized. With the possibilities for wonderful channels of information come problems dealing with property rights, privacy, copyright, and patent laws. Who owns the data that can circle the globe on the Internet? Sometimes it is hard to tell. The law dealing with electronic communication has not kept pace with the technology.

INTERNET TERMINOLOGY

One reason those new to computer research on the Internet may, at first, be intimidated is because some of the terminology is unfamiliar. Old guard Internet veterans quickly can spot a newbie. It's a bit like showing up for a sand lot baseball game and not knowing that three strikes mean you're out. There you might be set straight, but on the Internet, because no one can see that bewildered or hurt look on your face, you may be "flamed" with jeers and rude remarks for not knowing the rules.

Here are some terms that will help you understand the Internet.

ARCHIE, VERONICA, and **JUGHEAD** are tools for searching the huge libraries of information stored on the Internet. They can check what is where, then provide access to it. Alas, just like the comic book characters for whom they are named, they are also becoming extinct as the World Wide Web takes over.

ELECTRONIC MAIL or **E-MAIL.** This system allows you to send messages directly from your computer to another. It is an electronic post office — a very fast one. You can instantly send or receive multiple copies to or from many computers at the same time. All commercial online services (America Online, Prodigy, CompuServe, etc.) and local Internet service providers offer e-mail. (Chapter 10 gives more details.)

FILE TRANSFER PROTOCOL (FTP). This fetches programs and big documents from remote computers, called "sites," and allows you to download data to your computer from afar. If you need a password to enter a site, try using "anonymous," the standard sign-on for guest access.

FREE-NETS are regional community-oriented, electronic bulletin boards maintained by nonprofit organizations affiliated with the National Public Telecomputing Network (NPTN), an Ohio-based organization. It provides free, or at least inexpensive, access to the Internet, often through local governments, libraries, and schools within one local calling radius.

In some areas, libraries have used free-nets to allow home computer access to local library card catalogs, community referral data, public activities, and discussion groups. In most cases, free-nets do not offer Internet access to the public, but information is available to those with the necessary modem and communication software, using a local phone number. The Maryland state library system operates a program called "Sailor." It does offer access to the Internet at free or low-cost rates, becoming the first state library to offer this service.

In Ohio, using Cleveland Free-Net, donors who want to know more about where their charitable dollars are going can put their questions to United Way officials there. In other places, nonprofits can post information on their organizations on the local free-nets.

Watch for news of free-nets in your community. They are spreading quickly and may provide cut-rate Internet access for your organization. To find out about a free-net in your area, call the NPTN at 1-216-498-4050 for a list or e-mail to info@nptn.org.

FREQUENTLY ASKED QUESTIONS. Before you post a message or ask a question in listservs or newsgroups, read the Frequently Asked Questions (FAQs, pronounced facks) or general information for that group. FAQs are a means of answering the questions most commonly asked that arise again and again. More than likely, the things you wonder about have been answered. It's a good idea to print those answers for future reference and to check every couple of weeks for new FAQs.

GOPHER. Named for the rodent that burrows through the ground (and serves as the mascot for the University of Minnesota where Gopher originated) this tool enables you to tunnel quickly, or browse, menu-based Internet resources. You scan a series of lists until you find what you seek, then click to read it. Gopher knows where things are thanks to volunteers who spend time creating pointers to useful collections.

Although Gophers were very important in the history of the Internet, now many Gopher sites have been changed to World Wide Web sites for easier access. For serious research, however, many still prefer using Gophers for text downloading.

HOME PAGES are the fastest growing part of the Internet as businesses, nonprofit organizations, and individuals are setting up home pages or claiming space on the World Wide Web. Everywhere, it seems, you hear of another home page. A year or so ago, one felt naked without an e-mail address; now many organizations feel they must get a home page.

An e-mail address is just a mailbox; home pages are like your living room or reception area, with the door always open to those who wish to stop by. They provide sort of a table of contents of what you want to say about yourself or your organization. They can lead to a library of documents or available databases you have made available to those who stop by. A home page can link those who stop to other like-minded home pages.

When the Internet started, and as it grew, using the Internet for commercial gain was taboo. Now, perhaps unfortunately, profit is the primary motivation behind most of the World Wide Web home pages. Some require a fee to access data, others force users to view commercials that pay for the site. Some of the businesses with a home page just tell you what's available, like a catalog. Sadly, much of the Internet is like a television commercial, mostly without sound (though that's on the way!).

Those who stop by to look at a home page are counted as "hits." As businesses and others provide home pages, they often discover that hits are like window-shoppers. Many look; not all buy.

Despite that, the potential use of the Internet by nonprofits is great. Consider using a home page telling about your organization as a tool to attract donors and prospects from all those who browse the Internet. See listings of Web sites and examples of home pages in later chapters.

HTML is the programming language used to prepare a home page or document to display on the World Wide Web. It stands for HyperText Markup Language. In addition to text and pictures, hypertext links can be added so that browsers may jump directly to areas of interest with only a click of the mouse.

HTTP stands for HyperText Transfer Protocol, a behind-the-scenes system that delivers information via the World Wide Web. Users can enter a URL or click on a hypertext link to retrieve text or anything in digital format from a WWW server.

LISTSERVS and **MAILING LISTS**. These are e-mail-based discussion groups on a particular topic. Instead of being sent only to an individual on the list, messages are sent to a listserv address so they can be distributed to all who subscribe. (Look in Chapter 11 for examples of listservs with instructions for joining.)

MOSAIC appeared in 1993 and is an on-screen control panel browser that enables you to drive through the Web by pointing and clicking on graphical user interfaces. Documents look more like Windows screens than mail messages. With Mosaic aiding the World Wide Web, navigating the Net has become easier. Lucky for all of us, the system was developed at the University of Illinois in Champaign-Urbana with government funding, and the students gave it away. Millions of copies were downloaded from the University's National Center for Supercomputing Applications. Mosaic soon became a desired way to find information on the Internet and is now marketed commercially.

NETSCAPE is another very popular Internet navigation software package that allows you to cruise the Internet looking for World Wide Web sites with the click of your mouse. It retrieves text, graphics, or even video and sound clips and animation. It, also, became a huge commercial success as people needed some way to harness the massive Internet. By late 1995 it was the most-used way to access the Internet.

SLIP. It stands for Serial Line Internet Protocol, a way to enter the Internet through a provider offering World Wide Web access. With a SLIP account, now the most common type, organizations and even individuals can set up home pages to advertise themselves.

TELNET or **REMOTE LOGIN**. This permits you to access those remote computers from your own computer, as if your computer were a terminal connected to the remote computer. For example, you can search through library catalogs of holdings as if you were standing in the library lobby, using its terminal there. Some sites require an account or a password.

URL. Every web site has an address unique to itself, called a Uniform Resource Locator. It is in the form of resource type, followed by an Internet address, followed by a directory path. At first, Internet addresses look like hieroglyphics, but they really do follow a definite pattern. For example, an address beginning http:// indicates it is a World Wide Web site. Directories and subdirectories are divided by a slash (/).

USENET. This is a global network of computer bulletin boards, also called **NEWSGROUPS**, listed by subject matter and covering just about every conceivable topic, some rather kinky. They include messages that everyone who taps into the newsgroup can see. Then, the reader can respond by posting a message also. So the chat goes on. Newsgroups have been called electronic coffee klatches.

In newsgroups, the subject areas of the Internet are organized into hierarchies. Examples are: science (sci), recreation (rec), computers (comp), society (soc), and a miscellaneous category called alternate (alt).

WAIS. It stands for Wide Area Information Server and is a system to search Internet databases. You can do a keyword search using WAIS to retrieve matching documents and then read them.

WORLD WIDE WEB. This more advanced navigation system organizes its contents by subject matter to make it easier to establish links between computers around the world. Although the Internet is over 25 years old, the WWW began in 1991 at the European Particle Physics Laboratory (CERN) as a means to increase the efficiency of information exchange between scientists on the Internet.

With the WWW, nonhacker types could more easily use the Internet by browsing potential finds, then pointing and clicking. The Web operates as a graphics-intensive application running on top of the Internet's operating system. It, in fact, goes off to fetch the information you ask for—perhaps on the far side of the world.

It is difficult to overstate the importance of the Web for making resources available. Some people believe the Web is the most important advance in publishing since the printing press, because it permits anyone to publish documents for a global audience. And, best of all, the Web makes the document easier to find on the Internet than without it.

No one owns the Web, but anyone can own space on it. The space is cheap and, theoretically, infinite. In 1992 there were fewer than 100 sites on the WWW; by late 1995 there were around 200,000 sites. Not all sites are useful. In most cases they consist almost entirely of information that someone wants to give away, not what researchers traditionally have to pay for.

Forbes Magazine (October 23, 1995) stated that the Web is still tiny, in the world's grand scheme of things. It contains a fraction of 1percent of the world's publicly available data, though it triples in size each year. Anyone who assumes all the world's knowledge is on the World Wide Web and hopes to find it there will be sorely disappointed.

TRAFFIC JAMS ON THE INTERNET

One problem with any venture on the information highway is coping with traffic jams clogging your entrance. To understand the magnitude of the Internet, it now dwarfs any library in the world. The equivalent of the Library of Congress goes whizzing through the global computer network every few seconds, according to the *New York Times* (January 24, 1995.)

Trying to find that one tidbit of information amid the bulk can be a daunting task. If you are just cruising around for the fun of it, speed is no problem, except you might lose some sleep. If you depend on the Internet as a reference tool at the office, it is a more serious problem. It takes time. In fact, the World Wide Web has been referred to as the World Wide Wait.

There are ways to cope with this problem. Try getting information at off-peak hours. If your Internet provider requires many attempts to connect, consider changing providers. And ask before signing up how many customers can be handled simultaneously.

As the number of Internet users has roughly doubled every year since 1988, it is no surprise it is sometimes hard to get where you want to go. Another problem is that more and more networks love using graphics and sound, both hogging circuit capacity, by using fancy logos or mystery graphics that automatically display when you connect. Sometimes you can disable the images to speed things up a bit.

If you want to search networks in other parts of the world, consider doing it at their off-peak hours. You will get through faster.

You may be part of the traffic or clutter problem, subscribing to more mailing lists than you really need or allowing your e-mail boxes to get so cluttered no more mail will fit. If possible, set subscribed listservs to "digest" or, if only certain topics interest you, occasionally check the listserv archives for those keywords.

THOSE DARN ERROR MESSAGES

Sometimes, you won't get through at all. Here are some error messages that may appear just when you thought things were going well.

"Unknown or Failed DNS hookup" means there is a problem with the address entered or the system that locates that address.

"Unreachable" means part of the network is down.

"Too many connections. Try again soon" means the computer you want to enter is already filled to capacity.

"Timed out" or "not responding" or "refused" means the destination computer crashed or is unreachable for some reason.

"Timed out while reading" means there is a high volume of data to get through searching for a particular topic. Keep trying, or try at a less busy time.

"File is too large to display completely. Save to disk?" The file you want to view is too large to be seen on your screen. This occurs when your RAM can't hold any more. When this message is displayed, you are given the option of saving the file to disk. Do it. It is the only solution to this message.

"Error: User anonymous access denied." This means a site doesn't allow anonymous users to get access to their information because they may require paying a fee for the information or have licenses to take care of their own location only. There is no way around this situation.

GETTING ON

You are probably saying, "Okay, enough already! Just tell me how to get on. I'll figure it out as I go along,"

Okay, here's how. The short version. For a longer version, consult one of those all-inclusive, all-encompassing bibles the Internet experts have written. Once those folks had it all figured out, they had to do something with that knowledge. The solution was, of course, to write a book. In an article in *Fortune* on business uses of the Internet, the author concluded that the only people who were, so far, making money on the Net were those writing about it.

You need some equipment: an IBM-compatible personal computer (it doesn't even have to be a super powerful or expensive one, but having Windows software will make it easier) or Macintosh system. You will want a printer, a modem connected to a telephone line (a separate one, if possible), and communication software. For the Internet, the fastest modem you can afford is best, but get at least 14,400 bauds. If you are buying a new modem, go for 28,800 baud and things will move more quickly. That's all the equipment you need to begin.

If you're at a college or university, you are lucky. Almost all have Internet access already, and, best of all, they have bright young computer types who used computers in kindergarten who will come to your office. They will hook you up to the campus system and be there when you call in a state of panic because you think you've crashed the whole network. Don't worry, you probably can't do that.

If you are on your own, without a computer guru in sight, don't despair, you can get connected quite easily through a local Internet service provider. They can be found in any large or medium-sized North American city. Look for their ads in the daily newspaper's business section or the telephone yellow pages. Call and compare services and fee schedules. Be sure dial-in calls are local calls, to avoid long-distance charges. A flat monthly rate of around $25 is average, with 20 free hours online per month. Look for a low extra-time cost (around 50 cents an hour) so you won't have to worry as the minutes tick away. Ask if the company offers special rates for nonprofit organizations.

Ask also how many members and how many connections to the Internet they have, and remember that warning about traffic jams. A 30-to-1 ratio is normal, but 15-to-1 is better, for fast connection during busy times. Some can't keep up with the demand. Busy signals are usual if there are not enough access numbers.

Ask about technical support. When you're ready for it, can the company help you set up a home page on the World Wide Web? What about training? Free, or for an extra fee? Ask for references from other nonprofits using that company. Software and manuals should be part of the package. If you need on-site technical support, and you might, ask the service provider for recommendations.

There are other ways to connect to the Internet. Perhaps the easiest is through one of the commercial online services, now scrambling to outdo each other with Internet access. Those companies know they must offer access to keep their customers, so they have made it very easy. It takes only about ten minutes to load access software from Prodigy, Microsoft Network, America Online, and CompuServe. Call for their software, then just follow a few instructions, zap in a phone number to their service, and you're on. Most offer World Wide Web, Gopher, FTP, and WAIS access.

Those commercial online services have multiple access numbers and nodes across the country. Most have dedicated networks, and they are reliable. Busy signals are rare. Sudden disconnects are seldom and speed is consistent. Set it up and begin browsing or cruising immediately. Most offer the first month free of basic charges. Technical support is close, with many newcomer forums and instructions to copy and study. Those companies have been around a while and aim to please because the competition is steep.

Cost for a commercial online service is comparable to Internet service providers and, if you need help, someone is always close by, either online or with an 800 number to hold your hand. Using discipline, you should get by for $20-$30 per month for general services. If you use many of the extended reference services discussed elsewhere in this book, expect to pay much more.

HOW TO CREATE A HOME PAGE FOR
YOUR NONPROFIT ORGANIZATION

Many individuals, organizations, corporations, nonprofits, and government agencies are setting up home pages as a way to provide information to the public, through the World Wide Web. Because setting up a home page can be very low cost, or even no cost, it is a desirable option for even small organizations.

Nonprofits can use this vehicle to get the story of their organization out showing their concerns and activities to those who click on to the home page. Consider a home page, for example with basic information from your solicitation letter, going to whomever reads it. Those cruising the Net, may use keywords to find your listing or they can check one of the Internet location systems mentioned earlier. Other home pages could also provide a link to yours.

As details for secure transmission of credit card numbers, for example, are worked out, the home page may become as crucial to the fund-raising process as direct mail. It has been announced that Visa, MasterCard, and other credit card companies are meeting to discuss ways to make credit cards transactions more secure over the Internet. Until that happens, asking for contributions over the Internet is a bit shaky.

An example of the effectiveness of the Internet to an organization was shown after the Oklahoma City bombing in April 1995. Even though the American Red Cross had been on the Internet less than a month, people found its home page, though little promotion of the Internet address had been done. Incredibly, nearly 50,000 persons used their computers to get in touch with the American Red Cross. Many offered help and financial support by clicking on the "How You Can Help" icon on the home page.

The World Wide Web software allows groups to track how many people (or, actually, how many computers) checked into the home page. The technology shows from what country the inquiries came and which sections of the Web site were used. Those who wished to help the American Red Cross financially were advised to call toll-free telephone numbers or the phone numbers of local chapters.

Companies and nonprofit organizations wanting to set up a home page to distribute information (or advertise for clients or donors) can hire a company to create and service their Web home page at prices ranging from a low of $50 up to $500 a month. Even small nonprofit organizations and businesses can have home pages that link to other home pages. In fact, you do not have to ask permission to link your page to another page. Some of the home pages listed later link to each other, to distribute further information.

Costs for page-building used to be steep, but now software companies are releasing easy-to-use programs for creating home pages using HTML techniques. America Online, Prodigy, CompuServe, and others provide the software also. With that, it is possible for an organization to create its own home page or to seek computer students or other Internet-savvy people to volunteer their skills to set up a Web site. Many companies offer workshops and seminars telling why, and how, to establish home pages.

Look for listings in business sections of daily newspapers and in computer publications. John Seabrook in the *New Yorker* (October 16, 1995) wrote that your home page "shouldn't cost much. You ought to be able to find some neighborhood kid to do it for you, the way you'd find one to cut your lawn." Not far from the truth, it seems.

To get attention on the World Wide Web, experts say you need to keep the site pretty and constantly updated, because anything static will bore fast-cruising users. After you have your site, keep changing the graphics and text, or people will check in and quickly check out. For example, the American Red Cross site was updated almost daily. When dealing with hurricanes, earthquakes, or other fast-moving emergencies, the Internet connection proves its usefulness, as details can be added as they become available.

This gives just a glimpse of home page possibilities. As with all aspects of the Internet, there are dozens of books telling how to set up a home page and how to make it productive for your organization. Articles in nonprofit management journals are beginning to suggest all kinds of users for these new technologies.

GIVE THE INTERNET A TRY

Meanwhile, take advantage of what you already have. Use e-mail and listservs to communicate with your colleagues and to gain Internet experience. Both are good ways to begin your cyperspace journey. Jump in. Get your feet wet. You won't drown. Slosh around in the Internet and see what interests you. Figure out how to get where you want to go, then explore specific sites.

Check out the resources available on the Internet for nonprofit research listed in Chapters 12 and 13. I hope they will give you ideas for the kind of research you need to do. Remember, this is just a little of what is available. The beauty of the Internet, and its frustration, is that it always changes. New things become available but things disappear just as quickly. Just when you start depending on an information site, it may vanish into the clouds.

10

E-Mail: An Easy Way to Connect With Your Nonprofit Colleagues

"The Internet is just CB radio with typing."

Dave Barry

If the only lane you are taking on the information superhighway is e-mail, that's not too bad. Sure, you are missing a lot, but you are getting one very good feature. E-mail (electronic mail) is an electronic document sent from the sender's computer to the computer of one or more recipients. With some human intervention, of course.

As a user of e-mail, you can feel connected to the information superhighway. Having an e-mail address does give you a feeling of belonging, at least a bit, to this technological age. If it has not happened already, soon everyone will assume you have an e-mail address. It is where fax was a few years ago. Recently, America Online estimated that, each month, over 10 million pieces of e-mail zip through that system. Each month that number grows.

As time becomes crucial in our life (or we think it is), e-mail's speed is why regular U.S. Postal Service mail is labeled "snail mail" by e-mail users. It is part of the basic package, without additional charges, on most commercial online services, so it seems almost free. Cheaper than putting a stamp on an envelope; faster than walking to the mailbox. It is a powerful way to communicate.

E-mail is almost instantaneous. Nonprofits may want to use it for sending press releases to reporters, as most of them now have e-mail access. Organizations with offices in distant cities will discover e-mail as a super way to communicate with each other and to send documents back and forth. It is a wonderful way to communicate with those you met at the last conference.

Nonprofits are beginning to use e-mail very effectively to communicate with their members in this country or throughout the world. Sometimes the Internet or e-mail can take the place of a face-to-face meeting, thus saving considerable expense. It is an effective way to inform others about legislative alerts. Nonprofit executives can bring news of the organization, ask for suggestions, or poll members on controversial topics—all without leaving the office.

Current frustration with the ubiquitous voice mail makes e-mail all the more inviting. Instead of that merry-go-round that voice mail puts the caller through, with e-mail your message gets through instantly. With voice mail, even after you have carefully followed all instructions, you often find no human at the end, but yet another recorded voice asking you to leave a message.

Granted, with e-mail you may not get an answer right away, nor may your message be read instantly, but you are through. You are, so to speak, off the hook. You've delivered the message. Period. Unlike a regular phone call, e-mail does not require two busy people to be simultaneously engaged in the conversation. Both don't have to be at, or near, their telephone. In fact, you do not even have to consider the time factor. East coast persons no more have to wait until the west coast wakes up. Zap an e-mail message, and it will be there waiting when the recipient gets to the office and logs on to the computer.

E-mail often eliminates "small talk," as it has a certain speed element. Deliver the message, then get on with your life. This is its advantage, but it may also be its fault. The human element can be missing. Where is the human voice inflection, the discussion about the family, or even the weather? What is your take on the receiver's mood or reaction to what you've just said? You can't tell.

E-mail is a way to communicate and a way to cruise the world and talk to persons you have never met. You can ask questions, get advice, or discuss a topic with persons who may, or may not, be knowledgeable about the topic. It's up to you to decide that. Information through e-mail, or over the Internet, comes with no guarantee of quality.

Electronic advice from unknown persons may be about as reliable as stock information picked up at the water fountain. (It's different with information over online research services. You know who compiled the database and their reputation follows the data wherever it goes, regardless of the medium.)

E-Mail: ... Connect with your Nonprofit Colleagues

Getting an e-mail address is easy. First, you must have a modem and communication software connecting your personal computer to a telephone line. Then e-mail is available through an organization's connection to the Internet or through a commercial online service: CompuServe, America Online, Prodigy, MCI Mail, Genie, AT&T EasyLink, SprintMail, or Microsoft Network.

If your nonprofit office is a part of a university, or research facility, more than likely you have Internet access, though perhaps you have not used it. Check with your campus computer lab for details. By tomorrow you could be zapping messages to others.

E-MAIL ADDRESSES

Each commercial online service or Internet gateway access service has a distinctive type of address. The address may look more complicated than it is. The address is a set of commands that routes your message through a series of networks until it reaches the intended recipient, anywhere in the world. An e-mail address, like a postal address, is just a means of locating the person being contacted.

CompuServe, for example, uses a series of digits separated by a comma: 12345,678. America Online uses screen names chosen by the user when joining.

Internet addresses have two parts: the user ID and the host domain, divided by @. That tells what kind of organization owns the connection. The second half ends with these initials: "com" for commercial sites, usually research facilities at corporations or commercial online users; "gov" for nonmilitary government agencies; "edu" for educational sites, such as universities; "mil" for military sites; "int" for international organizations; "net" for networks through which e-mail must pass; or "org" for noncommercial or nonnetwork organizations.

You decode an Internet address from right to left. It goes from the larger group or network, down to the individual. Sending an address via the Internet from a commercial service such as CompuServe requires the up-front command Internet: followed by the individual address.

Sending to a CompuServe subscriber from Internet, for example, would look like this: 12345.678@compuserve.com. The comma between digits becomes a period and the name of the commercial service goes after the @ sign. E-mail to America Online or Prodigy follows a more routine pattern. It uses the screen name and then the service, like this: JDoe@aol.com or JDoe@prodigy.com. Check your individual online service for instructions.

Commercial services offer a generous, sometimes unlimited, number of e-mail messages per month for the basic subscription price of around $10. After the free number of messages allowed each month, additional messages sometimes are charged by the number of characters. Services such as fax, hard-copy mail, return receipts, mail alert, letterhead faxes when away from the office, and fax storage are offered by some companies.

In all cases, you can e-mail any others on the same service, using a member directory to find their number, or to others using an Internet gateway. Occasionally there is a "postage due" notice when mail is received from another vendor or the Internet, but it usually costs less than a 32-cent stamp. Most Internet connections don't limit number of e-mail uses per month. If you use e-mail a lot, it may be the least expensive way to communicate. Don't despair if your system seems a bit "technologically challenging" at first. Soon it will be as easy as stamping that old-fashioned envelope.

Most e-mail software allows you to make your own e-mail address directory by adding new numbers as you wish or by capturing the numbers of messages sent to you. Making your own address book is about the only way to keep track of your e-mail acquaintances. Usually there is a button in the communications software saying something like Add Sender to Address Book. Having already captured the sender's e-mail address, when you answer the e-mail letter you only have to click on that e-mail name or address. You can also use the convenient automatic reply feature to send an immediate answer.

Sometimes, the easiest way to get the e-mail address for someone with whom you wish to communicate is to call him or her on the telephone and ask for it.

There is no directory—like a universal phone directory for all e-mail addresses. It might fit on a CD-ROM, but it would require many phone-book-sized publications. There are other reasons why there is no universal directory. As the Internet is such a loose network of networks, it would be almost impossible to keep a directory up to date, as users change jobs or locations. Because of the lack of standards within the Internet, there is also no standard for a directory. In fact, there is no central office (like the telephone company) with whom to communicate about address changes.

There have been, and continue to be, worries about security and privacy on such an unstructured network as the Internet. Most users require a password or name code, within the organization's address, and most don't want the password known, even within the local network. Treat your password as you do your bank personal identification number.

Having said that, there are some ways to find e-mail users. Within the commercial services, it is possible to find others on the same service. For example, on CompuServe you need just the name, plus city or state, to find the CompuServe address. But that works only for CompuServe. For the bigger world of the Internet, check Ed Krol's "Finding Someone" chapter in his *The Whole Internet User's Guide & Catalog*. Krol gives some techniques for finding an individual's e-mail address.

As there have been print directories for mail addresses of the rich and famous, now there is a comparable *E-Mail Addresses of the Rich and Famous* by Seth Godin. (Addison-Wesley, $7.95) Don't count on it as a reliable source. Many people change their addresses if they get too much e-mail. (So can you. Contact your online service.)

One rather astonishing feature of e-mail is the strange route it takes to get from the sender to the addressee. When you get a message and print it out, the route it took is shown and may take more than half a page. Ignore it. Just as you don't have to know that your first-class letter that went by plane to San Francisco stopped off at airports in Cleveland, Minneapolis, and Denver, it doesn't really matter how the Internet message got to you. It just does. Amazing.

Unlike a letter going through the post office, or even a telephone call, you can't be completely sure of e-mail's security. If security or privacy is important, don't use e-mail. Or use it very carefully. If a message cannot be delivered, it is returned; sometimes it ends up where you don't expect it to, and others could read it. Passwords can be compromised. The most important point in making sure your messages get where you want, and nowhere else, is to be sure you use the correct address. It is easy to make typing mistakes. With e-mail, a comma is different than a period, and the number one and the letter l are not the same. The Internet expects you to be a perfect typist. It does not forgive mistakes. Even little ones.

Anything that is in digital form—software, sounds, graphic files—can be attached to an e-mail message. Some companies send their software updates via e-mail, at less cost than through the postal service. Software from the commercial services makes sending and receiving mail easy. Most use the inbox/outbox concept for managing mail. You can create a message offline, then load mail into your outbox, to be sent when you go online. Or you can create letters in your own word processing software, copy, and then "paste" them into the e-mail communication software.

As it arrives, incoming mail is dumped into your electronic inbox at your online service. When you go online, you get a message telling messages are waiting. On America Online, a voice says you have mail. (It's a bit spooky, but soon you get used to him. He also tells you good-bye when you sign off.) On CompuServe, a little mailbox appears in the upper right corner, with a message telling the number of waiting messages.

Once online, you can put the new messages into your inbox (with a push of a key or a touch of the mouse) to read at your leisure while offline. That way, the minutes are not ticking away while you read your mail.

Is there something on your mind you'd like to tell the President or Vice President? Do it with e-mail. Remember, though, your e-mail address goes with your message. When reelection time comes, you may get your personal e-mail response asking for a contribution and your vote. In 1993, when the e-mail addresses were first announced, messages poured in—more than 700 a day. Sometimes those writing got a canned answer, sometimes not. Don't be a silent majority. E-mail your views.

America Online — Clinton PZ
CompuServe — 75300,3115
Internet — President@whitehouse.gov
— Vicepresident@whitehouse.gov

Where you are in the country will depend on whether or not e-mail is economical. If you have to pay a toll, or long-distance charge, to connect to the online service, the cost adds up. Even then, using e-mail may be economically sound. Creating a message offline, then sending it online takes only seconds. Much less than a long-distance voice call would take. If a two-way conversation is not required, e-mail works well. When the answer comes back, you will again have to pay the toll charge to get online to claim the message.

In areas where access to an online service requires a long-distance toll charge, it is wise to investigate the most economical ways to dial into Internet access. Your service provider should be able to give you accurate information. Many now have toll-free 800 connection numbers.

With electronic mail, it is as easy to send a message to a group of people as to send it to a single person. This is called a mailing list. Your message can be coded so it goes to all addresses on the list. These mailing lists, also called listservs, are an important part of a nonprofit organization's use of electronics. Refer to the next chapter for more on this subject, plus a list of the most useful listservs for those in the nonprofit community. It is easy to subscribe to listservs. Once connected, a crush of useful information will be on the way to your computer. Like magic.

Electronic mail has features not known with postal mail. One is the already-mentioned reply feature. With most Internet or commercial online software, you can send a reply back to the sender without recopying the sender's address. Most services include the original letter, or selected parts, with the reply, if you want.

Sending "carbon copies" with e-mail is simple. You can put several addresses in the TO field and all will get a copy. Sometimes, it is useful to designate the person for whom the letter is intended, then indicate those who should get copies for reference only. For this, use the CC code. Sometimes you may wish to send copies but not let all who receive the message know who else got a copy. Use the BCC code (for blind carbon copies).

Now that e-mail addresses are as popular as fax machines, it seems logical that your business cards should include your e-mail address. It could put you in direct contact with 60 million (more or less) other e-mail users, according to the Electronic Messaging Association (EMA) in Arlington, Virginia. What used to look like ancient hieroglyphics now looks quite normal wherever the e-mail address appears. Now it shows you are on the cutting edge of business communication.

Once you begin to use electronic mail, you may want to get more detailed information from your campus or organization's computer technicians. One thing is for sure. You will like communicating by e-mail.

BULLETIN BOARDS

A further extension of the electronic communication concept are Bulletin Board Systems (BBS). These serve, to some extent, like a cork board where you could post a note to be read by those who walked by and paused to read it. Instead of cork, the messages appear on the computer screens of all who log into the bulletin board system.

The first BBS was created in 1978 so that those with incompatible computers could still communicate through a common dial-up host computer. By 1993 there were over 53,000 dial-up systems operating in this country, bringing people, using their computers, together for information of common interest.

BBSs are the true grass roots of electronic networks. Each is run by a system operator (called a sysop) who runs the system from home or office. This person has the host computer, to which individuals dial in for postings. A BBS can be set up almost anywhere. It requires no enhanced phone services, no Internet registration, or special cable connections. In many communities, this is a preferred way to get information out to residents about meetings, services, and events.

11

Listservs and Mailing Lists: Party Lines on the Internet

> *"We are at the center of a thing that is at least as big as Gutenberg. It is a change in the way we look at information, think about information, and trade in it."*
>
> Paul Hilts, *Publishers Weekly*

Are you old enough to remember telephone party lines? The telephone call was to one person but the whole neighborhood listened in. Wouldn't it be wonderful if there were party lines on the Internet? Well, actually, there are. They're called mailing lists or listservs. One message can be read by thousands and it's not even frowned upon.

When you begin using e-mail, it is only a matter of time before you discover electronic mailing lists. Once you know how to subscribe to a listserv, you can fill your electronic mailbox to overflowing, every day, with topics on almost every subject. But do you really want to? Remember, any kind of mail takes time to read and so does e-mail, no matter how interesting.

To get on a listserv of your choice, all you have to do is send off a subscribe command, and—presto—you begin to get lots of messages.

Generally, listservs have two addresses. One is the address you use to subscribe, change, or quit the list. The other is the address you use to send e-mail to the hundreds, or even thousands, on that listserv.

Electronic software needed to process a mailing lists is called listserv (thus, that name), majordomo, or listproc. It automatically processes a user's request. Because there is seldom any human intervention in the subscription process, you need to follow the sign-on directions exactly. If you deviate from what they expect, computers are not forgiving. Don't confuse listserv software by giving additional information, even including your e-mail address, unless asked. In most cases, that is picked up automatically. Don't type a polite thank you or say how delighted you are to be a part of this exciting electronic age. The computer really doesn't care.

Once connected to a listserv, you will receive a lengthy welcome message with instructions and information on appropriate behavior. Print it out and keep it close for future reference.

Listservs are possible because it is as easy to send a message to a group of people at one time as to a single person. Subscribers receive all messages posted from other subscribers. It can be a bit overwhelming! In fact, for those who love mail and love to chat, it's as addicting as a soap opera. For them, a day without checking for e-mail messages is almost impossible. Some go to the office on their days off; others gain access with their home computer.

It is not unusual to log on and discover 20, 30, or 40 mail messages waiting. Go away for a few days without checking and, when you come back, your electronic mailbox is overflowing. If the mailbox held paper, you might need a crane to pull it out of the mailbox. Like any mail, some is interesting, some is not. With a bit of listserv experience, you learn to detect what to read based on the subject heading. Delete everything else.

Luckily, it is easy to subscribe, to cancel, or to change listserv service. Because of the large number of messages posted, many listservs have a "digest" feature. With that, you get one message that combines all daily postings, instead of many separate messages. My advice: Subscribe to a listserv on a subject of interest, read all the postings for a week or two, then either ask for the digest, or be prepared to spend a lot of time reading your e-mail. If the topics never interest you, use the instructions to unsubscribe.

Most commercial services have online connect charges, so while online retrieve the messages quickly and zap them into your system's in-basket or to a download file on your hard disk, to be read offline.

The best feature of a listserv is the way strangers help strangers. Ask a question or ask for advice about a reference resource and someone will know the answer and share it. This is surely the human element on the information superhighway. Human interactions happen all the time, and though the persons may never meet, they become online colleagues.

Here are examples of listservs of particular interest to those working with nonprofit organizations. Listserv addresses (just like addresses on the Internet) have a way of changing or vanishing. If these addresses are no longer valid, try requesting the new address on one of the other listservs. Someone will know the current address. Guaranteed.

If you are subscribing from CompuServe, begin each address with INTERNET:, then proceed as described. Check with your service how to send messages to the Internet. If your communication software requires something in the subject area, just put a period, or anything, there. It doesn't get read so won't confuse the listserv software. Your e-mail address is taken from the message you send. This prompts an automatic reply saying you are subscribed with additional information. Listserv software is not case sensitive, but majordomo software operates with UNIX, which is case sensitive.

Let's begin our list with a well-established listserv used by a variety of nonprofit staff members. Procedures used with PRSPCT-L are similar to those used with other listservs.

PROSPECT RESEARCHERS

PRSPCT-L (pronounced "prospect el") is an unmoderated list provided as a forum for discussion of prospect research issues. It is intended to serve nonprofit and service organization researchers and educational development professionals. Areas of discussion include research resources, techniques, ethics, job announcements, conference details, and office management. Many vendors, or suppliers of nonprofit-related items, read the postings but are forbidden from advertising their own products.

While information on individual donors is usually not asked for or distributed, it is not unusual for researchers to post questions about foundations, biographical directories, upcoming conferences, techniques for rating prospects, or how to distribute research work within the office. PRSPCT-L messages sometime carry a warning about very expensive reference resources, with words such as "not worth the price." That message may be answered by someone who likes the book and gives a different view, as the thread of postings continues.

To join PRSPCT-L, e-mail this message.

TO: listserv@bucknell.edu

MESSAGE: subscribe PRSPCT-L firstname lastname (that's *your* name)

PRSPCT-L is administered by Joe Boeke at Bucknell University in Pennsylvania. He began the list while in a previous research position in California. Although as list moderator, Joe makes no attempt to stop spirited conversation, he does keep the more than 1,000 subscribers to PRSPCT-L on track. When necessary, he posts messages on what is, and what isn't, appropriate on PRSPCT-L.

To change to a daily digest version of PRSPCT-L, send this message:

TO: listserv@bucknell.edu

MESSAGE: set PRSPCT-L mail DIGEST

If you will be away from your computer for a few days or longer, you may wish to send a "POSTPONE" message as above, using postpone instead of DIGEST. This will disable mail delivery to your address until you change mode again, and the messages will not fill your e-mail box to overflowing. When you return, resubscribe to the above address with:

MESSAGE: set PRSPCT-L mail ACK

To end your subscription, send:

TO: listserv@bucknell.edu

MESSAGE: signoff PRSPCT-L

Remember, there are two addresses for most listservs. One handles administrative matters such as adding or removing subscribers from a list. In this case, it begins with "listserv." The other begins with the name of the listserv group, PRSPCT-L. It posts the message to all list subscribers. A common mistake is to confuse the two addresses.

To post a message for all on the list to read, use this address:

TO: PRSPCT-L@bucknell.edu

Your subscription to PRSPCT-L brings a very useful *Internet Prospector* issue each month by e-mail. It features new Internet sites discovered by those who have found research treasures there.

If all this sounds confusing to someone new to this electronic mail world, be assured, there is help available. If you can get past the sign-up, and you can, you will be greeted and made to feel welcome by Joe Boeke. If needed, send e-mail to him at BOEKE@bucknell.edu.

If you want more information on PRSPCT-L, including frequently asked questions, send:

TO: listserv@bucknell.edu

MESSAGE: help

Here are other listservs of interest to nonprofit groups. Most use similar commands for subscribing. Once subscribed, you will get an e-mail message with specific instructions for that listserv.

ADVOCACY FOR THE DISABLED

ADVOCACY is a mailing list to help people with disabilities by promoting discussion of health-care reform, employment, transportation, and civil rights issues. To subscribe:

> TO: listserv@juvm.stjohns.edu
>
> MESSAGE: subscribe ADVOCACY firstname lastname

ADVOCACY FOR PUBLIC LIBRARY ISSUES

PUB-ADV fosters discussion of all types relating to public libraries. It is open to library trustees, library directors, librarians, and board members of friends of libraries groups. To subscribe:

> TO: listserv@nysernet.org
>
> MESSAGE: subscribe PUB-ADV firstname lastname

ALTERNATIVE ENERGY

The Alternative Energy Discussion List provides a forum to discuss renewable and sustainable systems and alternative energy sources.

> TO: listserv@sjsuvm1.sjsu.edu
>
> MESSAGE: subscribe AE firstname lastname

ALUMNI

ALUMNI-L deals with alumni reunions and relations, mostly at colleges and universities. To subscribe:

> TO: listserv@brownvm.brown.edu
>
> MESSAGE: subscribe ALUMNI-L firstname lastname

ARTS MANAGEMENT

ARTMGT-L is for arts administrators and arts managers. To subscribe:

> TO: listserv@bingvmb.bitnet
>
> SUBJECT: subscribe ARTMGT-L firstname lastname

BUSINESS LIBRARIANS

BUSLIB-L is a listserv for business librarians, thus it is helpful for corporation and foundation research. To subscribe:

> TO: listserv@idbsu.idbsu.edu

> MESSAGE: subscribe BUSLIB-L firstname lastname

CHRISTIANS IN FUND RAISING

This listserv will discuss philanthropy issues from a Christian perspective. The name is "hilaros," a Greek word used in Second Corinthians 9:7 "For God loves a cheerful (hilaros) giver."

> TO: majordomo@mark.geneva.edu

> MESSAGE: subscribe HILAROS (no need for your name)

CORPORATE AND FOUNDATION RELATIONS

CFRNET-L is for those who work at nonprofit organizations with an interest in corporate and foundation relations. Subscribe to:

> TO: listserv@gibbs.oit.unc.edu

> MESSAGE: subscribe CFRNET-L firstname lastname

DONORS AND VOLUNTEERS

GIVING is a listserv for donors and volunteers to discuss wise giving and other issues about philantrophy. To subscribe:

"For Sale: Copier, Sharp, Commercial SF850, does 3 sides of paper, $99."

The St. Petersburg Times
(*PC Magazine*, May 16, 1995)

> TO: listproc@envirolink.org
>
> MESSAGE: subscribe GIVING

ESTATE PLANNING

ESTPLAN-L discusses techniques of estate planning and products of the financial services industry. It includes reports of recent IRS findings, court cases, and new legislation. To subscribe:

> TO: listserv@netcom.com
>
> MESSAGE: subscribe ESTPLAN-L firstname lastname

FUND RAISERS

FUNDLIST is a listserv for fund-raising professionals, many from universities and colleges, who discuss topics of interest. This may include annual campaigns, alumni surveys, major gifts, and planned giving. To join, send e-mail:

> TO: listproc@listproc.hcf.jhu.edu
>
> SUBJ: subscribe FUNDLIST firstname lastname

Another list of special interest to fund raisers and planned giving staffs is TALK-AMPHILREV. It's a fairly new list from the editors of *American Philanthropy Review* that plans to be a cross-over list on many related topics. Unlike many lists, this welcomes "tasteful" product information from vendors. To subscribe:

> TO: majordomo@tab.com
>
> SUBJ: subscribe talk-amphilrev

FUND RAISERS ON TECHNOLOGY ISSUES

Those fund raisers who want to discuss which software to use to track donors or to store information on donors might want to check out FUNDSVCS.

> TO: majordomo@acpub.duke.edu
>
> MESSAGE: subscribe fundsvcs

Where the Information Is

GENEALOGY

ROOTS-L discusses genealogical issues and gives techniques for those involved in this research either for their own ancestors and relatives or for those of their prime prospects. It also deals with surname queries and genealogical web sites. To subscribe:

TO: listserv@mail.eworld.com

MESSAGE: subscribe ROOTS-L firstname lastname

GRANT FUNDING

GNET-L is part of an online service from the U.S. Department of Health and Human Services. It provides information about applying for and administering grants from that agency, including training sessions for grant seekers. To subscribe:

TO: listserv@list.nih.gov

MESSAGE: subscribe GNET-L firstname lastname

GRANTS-L gives information about funding for international education and research. To subscribe:

TO: listproc@listproc.gsu.edu

MESSAGE: Subscribe GRANTS-L firstname lastname

INTERNATIONAL FUND RAISERS

INTFUND is for those interested in international fund raising. To subscribe:

TO: listserv@vm1.mcgill.ca

MESSAGE: subscribe INTFUND firstname lastname

JEWISH RESOURCES

A-Z ANNOUNCE is a mailing list designed to announce new Jewish and Judaism resources on the World Wide Web. Established in August 1995, the list welcomes users from around the world. To subscribe:

TO: majordomo@ort.org

MESSAGE: subscribe a-z announce

LIBRARY FUND RAISING

A listserv called FRFDS-L is devoted to fund raising and financial development in libraries. It was established by the Library Administration and Management Association (LAMA) from the American Library Association to cover all aspects of fund raising.

> TO: listserv@uicvm.uic.edu
>
> MESSAGE: subscribe FRFDS-L firstname lastname

Another, mostly for academic library development staff, is LIBDEV. To subscribe:

> TO: listserv@listserv.arizona.edu
>
> MESSAGE: subscribe LIBDEV firstname lastname

MAJOR GIFTS AND PLANNED GIVING

GIFT-PL, run by the National Commission on Planned Giving, is a listserv for development and planned giving officers, many at academic institutions. To subscribe, send e-mail, as above, to:

> TO: listserv@indycms.iupui.edu
>
> MESSAGE: subscribe GIFT-PL firstname lastname

MAJOR GIFT MANAGEMENT

GIFT-MGT offers discussion on managing planned gifts after the transaction has been completed by development staff. It includes topics such as prudent investment, fiduciary obligations, reporting, and tax compliance. To subscribe:

> TO: listserv@netcom.com
>
> MESSSAGE: subscribe GIFT-MGT firstname lastname

NONPROFIT ADVOCACY

When legislation comes before Congress that have an effect on nonprofit organizations, Let America Speak! distributes information through this moderated listserv. RTK-NET sends analyses, updates, and requests for action to subscribers. To subscribe, send an e-mail request:

TO: graysonj@rtk.net

MESSAGE: give your name, organization, phone number, and e-mail address

NONPROFITS AND THE INTERNET

This list began in late 1995 and promises discussion of how nonprofits can use the Internet to distribute their information with home pages, using the WWW for research, and other electronic techniques. To subscribe:

TO: listproc@nonprofit.net

MESSAGE: sub NONPROFIT-NET firstname lastname

OBITUARY LISTS

Nonprofit development researchers often need an obituary or a confirmation of death. GEN-OBIT offers a way to get current obits from around the United States and Canada. This list distributes obit information sent in by subscribers. They are asked to take a few minutes each day to record and submit obits from their local newspapers with a complete name, death date, and place of death for the deceased person.

Details on submitting information and searching the archives will come with your subscription acknowledgement. To subscribe:

TO: listserv@mail.eworld.com

MESSAGE: subscribe GEN-OBIT firstname lastname

PUBLIC RELATIONS PROFESSIONALS

PROFNET is a listserv for those doing public relations work in nonprofit organizations. It connects media outlets to academic experts and thus promotes the institution they represent. To subscribe:

TO: dforbush@ccmail.sunysb.edu

MESSAGE: INFORMATION

REFERENCE QUESTIONS
THAT STUMP LIBRARIANS

STUMPERS is a way to get answers to questions that have stumped the hometown librarians. If the librarian cannot find the answer, he or she will post the question and usually get an answer within a day. To subscribe:

TO: mailserv@crf.cuis.edu

To post messages, send to: stumpers-list@crf.cuis.edu

To contact the moderator: roslibrefrc@crf.cuis.edu

SEC REPORTS

EDGAR-INTEREST is for those interested in discussing issues relating to Internet distribution of SEC filings. As the Net became more used by those seeking this information, many consumer advocates campaigned to have company 10-Ks offered there. Their reasoning was if citizens paid with their taxes for the SEC to gather the information, why shouldn't it be made available free. Previously this had been available only through vendors who processed the data then sold it online or on CD-ROMs. To subscribe, e-mail to:

TO: majordomo@town.hall.org

MESSAGE: subscribe edgar-interest

U.S. NONPROFIT ORGANIZATIONS

USNONPROFIT-L is a listserv discussion group on issues facing nonprofit organizations and the sectors they serve. Sponsored by the Santa Barbara RAIN Network, it covers management, fund raising, grant resources, and building business/nonprofit partnerships. To subscribe:

TO: majordomo@rain.org

MESSAGE: subscribe usnonprofit-l

NEW DISCUSSION LISTS

New listservs appear on the Internet almost every day. So how do you find the one that might interest you? Those bright folks on the Internet have provided a way by listing new lists.

NEW-LIST was established as a central address to post announcements of new public mailing lists. It's useful for finding interesting lists on specific topics you may find of value. This new list information comes with a disclaimer from NEW-LIST. Announcements are edited with information from the original submitter, with no quarantee that they are what is stated. It's a "use-at-your-own-risk" kind of thing. But then, so is a lot on the Internet. To subscribe:

TO: listserv@vm1.nodak.edu

MESSAGE: subscribe NEW-LIST firstname last-name

For more information: listserv@vm1.nodak.edu

MESSAGE: get NEW-LIST readme

There are other ways to search on the World Wide Web for discussion lists. These searchable directories pick up new and somewhat obscure lists. Check these.

http://www.nova.edu/Inter-Links/cgi-bin/news-lists.pl

http://www.liszt.com

THE LISTSERV AS BACK FENCE

Subscribing to and using a listserv is a bit like talking to your colleagues at the water fountain or morning coffee pot, assuming all are engaged in similar work. Listservs have been called the back fence, the neighborhood bar, or the lunch counter of your profession. You can pick up a lot of information (or gossip) but you can also waste a lot of time with things that don't really affect your work.

Going through a day's postings may take an hour. Sometimes it will take even more, if you decide to reply to a message. Then, the time spent can go on and on as you look for replies to your reply. It's the beauty, or the downside, of this new technology. Probably both.

Most listservs have FAQs available for the e-mail asking. In most cases, send just a HELP message to the listserv moderator. Those answers tell how to post messages, in what format, and how to put an appropriate subject heading on your message. They tell how to reply, picking up comments from the first message, so readers will know to what you are responding. What they don't tell is how to separate the wheat from the chaff and to do it quickly—before the morning is gone.

When you subscribe, you may get an explanation of the colons and parentheses in messages that seem to make no sense. They are known as emoticons or smileys, used to show emotion in your e-mail message. In person, the expression on your face or the tone of your voice tell something of your intent. Without those markers, the true meaning may be lost. A smiley may help get your message across.

The basic smiley is this :-). Turn the page 90 degrees to the right and you see a "happy face." In an e-mail message this shows a joke or happiness. A frowning smiley is this :-(and it shows displeasure or unhappiness. :-V is a shout and :-ll shows anger. Put a little sarcasm or flirtation in your message with ;-).

Each listserv has a code of etiquette. Break that code and you may get flamed (the online version of scolded) or set straight. The danger often is that persons reading a message feel compelled to agree, sort of like nodding your head in a real conversation. The "me too" messages clutter up the mailings and contribute nothing. Such agreement at the water fountain may be appreciated, but not here. Even a "thanks for the help" message can get tedious if read by hundreds. Rather than bore hundreds, send an e-mail message only to the individual involved.

Another problem is when a reply should be sent to the individual posting the first message, seeking information, for example, and the person who replies sends it to everyone, via the listserv. It's a mistake most often made by beginners or by someone who falsely thinks all are interested in the answer.

Listservs are miniconferences you can attend without leaving your desk. Never before have persons been able to zip around the country (or world) with the ease offered by these electronic methods. It's an old idea, though. Samuel Morse, more than 150 years ago, said, "I see no reason why intelligence might not be instantly transmitted by electricity to any distance."

12

The Internet: What's On It for You?

"Does anyone actually know how to use the Internet" No, I don't think anybody does. The Internet is like God: You suspect it's there, but without a religion to organize it, it's difficult to access.

Well, the World Wide Web is sort of like that religion. The Web organizes the chaotic Internet into a comprehensible, and most awe-inspiring universe."

Jeanne Marie Laskas
Washington Post Magazine

Whether or not you decide to use the Internet in your nonprofit office depends on what it can do for you. Does it have the information you need or want? Can you find it? Can you use the networking and e-mail features to speed up your communication? Can you use the Internet to disseminate information about your organization to gain exposure and/or contributions? Would your organization benefit from its own home page?

The answer to those questions is an enthusiastic YES. Even if no new sites were added to the Internet (and you can be sure that new things are being added daily) it would be worthwhile to connect to the Internet as soon as possible. It is easy to do.

With the equipment mentioned elsewhere in this book and a connection to an Internet service provider or one of the consumer online services you have all you need to use Internet resources.

This chapter and the next will give Web sites for some of those resources. You may discover other sites—perhaps even more exciting than these. If so, share them with your colleagues through one of the listservs, depending on the subject of your discoveries. Internet addresses change often. If one of these addresses no longer gets you where you want to go, don't despair. Ask others on a mailing list for the new address. Someone will probably provide it.

Evidence that things change quickly on the Internet is the change from Gopher access to the World Wide Web. In 1991, the Gopher navigator of the Internet was developed, and by mid-1994 there were about 7,000 Gopher sites online. Most were at colleges and universities, research institutions, government agencies, and libraries. Gophers allowed you to find information without knowing complicated addresses or commands. With it, you could keep track of favorite places with a bookmark menu for easy return.

Next, along came the World Wide Web with picture-based browsers (such as Lynx, Mosaic, and Netscape) doing what Gophers had done, only better. Soon Gopher addresses changed to the now familiar WWW addresses (http://). With the Web, access was made easier, but some of the most useful materials are still best found by Gopher, especially text-heavy documents. Like the adaptable creatures they are in real life, Gophers on the Internet will probably change and become more user friendly as time passes. If not, they still will have played an important part in the history of the Internet.

ONLINE ASSISTANCE WITH SEARCH ENGINES

Still feeling a bit shaky about all of this? Do you feel you're wandering around a huge grocery story with no shopping list? You're not alone. Everyone expects that newcomers (those before-mentioned newbies) will need some help. Even experienced searchers need help locating Web sites. Search engines to the rescue.

Search engines are ways to find your way around the Internet, using various methods to look for information with keywords you provide. Other words for search engines are "spiders" or "robots" because they wander through Web sites, picking up relevant terms for identification. Because of the vast field of knowledge, it is wise to use very specific terms to pinpoint your search. (Example: BROCCOLI, not VEGETABLES.)

Just to see what is available on the Internet for nonprofit organizations, try a couple of the search engines listed here. Most ask you to supply a keyword to search. Try fund raising, nonprofits, volunteers, philanthropy, and charity to see how they work. You will be amazed, as I was, at the variety of home pages found on those topics with the Internet addresses listed. Not all are useful, but some are.

Perhaps the best known search engine is Yahoo. It took two students at the Stanford University to figure out there must be a better way to find things on the Internet than by chance encounter. They devised a very popular index, called the Yahoo Home Page, with about 40,000 (and now many more) links to almost every subject. It is sort of a table of contents to the Internet with descriptive brief abstracts. Try it, but don't be surprised if you don't get through. Yahoo gets a quarter of a million visits daily. It's free, but has some corporations that pay dearly for advertising space there.

http://www.yahoo.com

With Yahoo, you can find Usenet links, FAQs, search tools, directions, and a list of Usenets.

http://www.yahoo.com/News/Usenet

————

The World Wide Web Worm indexes pages across the Internet using keywords within a URL address and home pages. Good instructions make this fairly easy to use.

http://www.cs.colorado.edu/home/mcbryan/WWWW.html

————

MetaCrawler searches other search engines in a piggyback fashion. This may be the wave of the future. With it, you can search for phrases as well as single words, so you get fewer incorrect hits.

> http://www.metacrawler.com

Open Text is another spider that can search for phrases because it indexes every word.

> http://opentext.com

WebCrawler is America Online's proprietary spider, but it can be used by anyone on the Net.

> http://www.webcrawler.com

Here's one more. Altavista is a recent addition to the search engine family. It indexes over 16 million Web pages with 8 billion words.

> http://altavista.digital.com

Despite the fact that there are very popular search engines to thousands—no, millions—of Web pages, available for free on the Internet, a commercial program offers its service for a fee. If you want to find information on the Internet quickly and conveniently, InfoSeek searches the full text of Web pages and messages from 10,000 Usenet newsgroups. You will need a WWW browser to use it.

It costs $9.95 a month for 100 searches and retrievals, or, for occasional users, $1.95 per day for eight transactions. For more information, e-mail to: info@infoseek.com or fax: 1-408-986-1889.

InfoSeek allows a free "guided tour" so you can run some of your own queries on a demo collection without registering for an account.

> http://www.infoseek.com

———

Okay, that's fine for those who have lots of time to play around online and want to find information on dogs, cats, or potbellied pigs. Aren't there ways to find Internet sites of special interest to nonprofit organizations? Yes there are.

Giving credit where it is due, much of the following information is from the *Internet Prospector*, a monthly electronic newsletter that comes to subscribers to PRSPCT-L. (See details about this listserv in Chapter 11). Produced by volunteer editors and Net surfers, it includes Internet sites, tips, and research ideas. Once subscribed to PRSPCT-L, you receive instructions to find back issues of the *Internet Prospector*.

Anyone working with (or writing about) the Internet discovers that it is indeed a net, or maybe a jungle. Some Internet sites listed in these chapters were found by luck. Others were taken from articles in nonprofit, computer, and business periodicals; association newsletters; daily newspapers; online publications; and Internet guides.

GENERAL INFORMATION ON NONPROFITS ON THE INTERNET

Internet information for nonprofit organizations is growing daily. Realizing this, many Internet-savvy individuals have done the heavy lifting so you don't have to. They have assembled home pages with direct links to vast amounts of information. Once connected to those home pages, you can click on a listed site and be connected there.

Some of these home pages were created by individuals within a nonprofit organization as a public service to others. Some have been created by commercial enterprises as a way to let others know about their products and services, but they also provide information and links to other home pages. I suggest looking at some of these sites and reading their tables of content. It will give you an idea of the variety of information on the Internet.

Northwestern University has a "Development Research Page" created and maintained by researcher Lance Hill. It includes an online version of the newsletter from the APRA-Illinois chapter and useful fund-raising and research tips. Examples are a database of tax assessor offices nationwide and the procedure to determine fair market value from assessed value. It links to EDGAR (see details in the next chapter) and sites for stock quotes. Check it out at:

http://pubweb.acns.nwu.edu/~cap440/

David Lamb from the University of Washington has a "Prospect Research Page." It's filled with excellent material and is updated as new research sites are developed. His page, as many others do, offers link access to many other sites, many listed here. With these links, once you are at this home page, you can click on the listed Net site and go directly there.

http://weber.u.washington.edu/~dlamb/research.html

Butler University's "Virtual Prospect Research" home page from its Office of University Advancement, done by Martha Murphy, lists good research sites with links to them.

http://www.butler.edu/~mmurphy/index.html

"Philip A. Walker's Home Page" is a catalog of Internet sites for nonprofits, many of interest to United Way of America-related agencies. This is a good site to check for recently added Web sites.

http://www.clark.net/pub/pwalker/home.html

"Philanthropy Related Links" from Duke University is an index to sites of interest to nonprofits compiled by Peter Tavernise. It lists grant-giving foundations, nonprofit organizations, and useful resources. The "Meta-Index of Non-Profit Organizations on the Web," formerly run by Ellen Spertus from the Massachusetts Institute of Technology is available here. It is a guide by subject to many categories relating to nonprofit work, such as human rights, civil liberties, the environment, and animal rights.

http://www.duke.edu/~ptavern/Pete.Philanthropic.html

http://www/duke.edu/~ptavern/Pete.meta-index.html

"Internet Resources for Non-Profit Public Service Organizations" is a service from the University of Michigan, School of Information and Library Studies, compiled by Sarah Nesbeitt and Richard Truxall. It covers a wide range of issues with special emphasis on information relating to human service programs.

http://asa.ugl.lib.umich.edu/chdocs/nonprofits/nonprofits.html

---

Impact Online is a nonprofit agency dedicated to increasing the public's involvement with nonprofit organizations through the use of electronic technology.

http://infobase.internex.net:80/impact/

Inez Bergquist has been active in the research field for many years. Her home page includes tips for prospect researchers with lists of reference books and consulting services from Waltman Associates. The page includes an individual and recipient index to the *Philanthropic Digest*. The Digest, now published by APRA, includes grants of more than $10,000 given by individuals.

http://www.umn.edu/nlhome/g248/bergq003/wa/

———

Putnam Barber' Home Page offers files of frequently asked questions about nonprofit organizations. It is arranged by subjects such as fund raising, boards, management, marketing, grants, and office automation. It includes a link to other Internet resources for nonprofits.

http://www.eskimo.com/~pbarber/

———

Perhaps you are interested in how fund raisers in the United Kingdom do their work. Check into this excellent site from Howard Lake of Amnesty International—UK. It links to other fund raising home pages.

http://www.city.ac.uk/~bh543/fundraising.html

———

And for Canada? Yes, there is a similar site provided by a leading Canadian provider of resources for nonprofits. It links to a directory of nonprofits and other foundation sites.

http://www.charityvillage.com/cvhome.html

GRANTS AND GRANTMAKERS ON THE INTERNET

Many groups provide Internet lists to grant opportunities. These are just a few examples. It is a good idea to download one of the guides listed below for more complete lists.

The Foundation Center has long been the chief source of information on foundations and the grants they give. Their print directory and access to grant information through DIALOG have pointed to available funding for many nonprofits. Now some information from the Center is on the Internet, although not most basic foundation and grant information from its directory. The Center hopes to find ways, for a fee, to make that available in the future. Meanwhile, it gives locations of Foundation Center libraries and cooperating collections, tips on seeking grants, and a catalog of its publications.

http://fdncenter.org

Philanthropy News Digest, a summary of news on philanthropy from the print media, is from the Foundation Center at this site.

> http://fdncenter.org/philmain.html

———

Off into the future, perhaps in 1998, the Federal Government promises to have up and running Internet access to Internal Revenue Service foundation annual reports (IRS-990). All tax-exempt foundations and nonprofits must file a report with the IRS each year to detail their financial picture. It includes salary of executives and spending patterns of money entrusted to the organization. Having those reports readily available will be an easy way to get information on a foundation. This project will eventually require that foundations file their reports electronically for easier dissemination to the public. Watch for details.

———

The Council of Foundations has about 1,300 members, including over 400 community foundations. It describes the types and roles of foundations and offers assistance with their giving programs. The Council, located in Washington, DC, can be accessed at this site.

> http://www.cof/org/

———

"A Grant Getter's Guide to the Internet" by James Kearney of the University of Idaho College of Education provides where-to-look data. It is especially good for those seeking education grants. It includes extensive federal grant information and foundation/private resources. Internet address sites are given.

> http://gopher.uidaho.edu:70/1s/e-pubs/grant

This guide can be downloaded from several nonprofit home pages. Watch for its title in the tables of content.

———

The University of Michigan has a "Resources for Grant Writing on the Internet" home page developed by Eva Lyford. It tells where to find information on grants, contracts, and fund raising.

http://www.umich.edu/~trinket/Resources_for_Grant. html

———

Grants Alert, an online project from the University of Utah's Office of Sponsored Projects, gives periodic updates on grant information from state, local, corporate, and foundation sources. The gopher can tunnel through a variety of Internet databases and documents to find subject headings.

gopher to: gopher.cc.utah.edu

———

ArtsNet includes funding information for those searching the Internet for grants to support the arts.

http://artsnet.heinz.cmu.edu/DevelopmentResources/

———

Many foundations now list data about themselves with home pages. An example of an excellent foundation home page is from the John D. and Catherine T. MacArthur Foundation. It tells about the foundation and what grants are available in specific fields and how to apply for them.

gopher://gopher.macfdn.org:3016/

———

Look in the next chapter for information on how to find federal grants on the Internet.

HOME PAGES OF ASSOCIATIONS, NETWORKS, AND NONPROFIT ORGANIZATIONS

An example of association presence on the Internet is the Association of Professional Researchers for Advancement. Its home page tells about that organization and its activities.

It includes a list of the officers and board members, conference schedules, registration, and access to APRA's officers. Job postings for prospect researchers are here. This home page is maintained by David Lamb of the University of Washington whose own "Prospect Research Page" is listed previously.

> http://weber.u.washington.edu/~dlamb/apra/APRA.html

Internet Nonprofit Center offers a central and searchable register of Internet Web pages provided by nonprofit organizations. Its goal is to provide "fast, easy, and free access to information about nonprofits." It is sponsored by the American Institute of Philanthropy and staffed by volunteers. The center aims to help individual donors and volunteers find information and evaluation of nonprofits.

Basic information, not specific to any one nonprofit, is provided by the Center. This can provide information and advice about giving to nonprofits and volunteering. It has financial information online for more than 10,000 charities, registered in several states. Most information is from charity registration forms. It has FAQs and a downloadable "donor defense kit."

> http://www.human.com:80/inc/

The National United Service Agencies is a collection of national charitable organizations and international service agencies that provide information on organizations that have Web pages.

> http://www.charities.org/

There are listings of American universities with Web pages. Try these sites, and be aware that the number grows daily.

> http://www.clas.ufl.edu/CLAS/american-universities.html

http://www.mit.edu:8001/People/cdemello/univer.html

———

ReliefNet provides information on international relief efforts and provides a way for those groups to use Internet technology. It connects potential donors with those groups, using a pledge option that tells the appropriate organization to get in touch with the donor.

http://www.relief.org:2805/reliefnet.html

———

Many agencies working to relieve hunger around the world are connected on HungerWeb.

http://www.hunger.brown.edu/hungerweb/

———

The American Red Cross is America's largest humanitarian organization, helping over 40 million people each year. As previously mentioned, the Red Cross used this site to good advantage during the Oklahoma City bombing followup to provide information about the disaster and to solicit contributions.

http://www.crossnet.org

———

InterAction is a coalition of agencies dealing with international development, relief and refugee assistance, and humanitarian aid to the world. It strives to ease suffering and strengthen people's abilities to help themselves.

http://www.vita.org/iaction/iaction.html

———

The Institute for Global Communications (IGC) is the umbrella under which PeaceNet, EcoNet, ConflictNet, and LaborNet reside.

http://www.igc.apc.org
http://www/igc.apc.org/index.html

Once there, you can select from the main menu which network you want.

_____

Envirolink Network is the largest online environmental information service in the world, connecting interested workers in 98 countries. All services of this network are free.

http://envirolink.org:/start_web.html

gopher://envirolink.org:70/11/.EnviroOrgs/.inc

_____

The World Crisis Network was developed by Food for the Hungry, a Christian organization committed to overcoming global hunger and poverty. This Web site tells of the group's work.

http://www.fh.org/

_____

Volunteers in Technical Assistance (VITA) operates to support development work around the world with an information resource service.

http://www.vita.org/

_____

The Global Electronic Network for AIDS and HIV-positive issues includes treatment information, a guide to research and counseling, gay men's health treatment issues, and pediatric AIDS information,

gopher: hivnet.org

http://www.hivnet.org

_____

The Web's stop for people with disabilities is WebAble. It includes a quarterly newsletter, a directory of listservs, product catalogs, and information from research papers.

http://www.webable.com/

_____

The Web of Addictions is dedicated to providing information about alcohol and drug addictions. This links to other resources and posted information on the Internet with news, articles, and announcements.

http://www.well.com/user/woa

Many church headquarters have Web sites. Here is one that was judged "informative and clearly written" when listed in *NetGuide* magazine (October 1995). It gives basic information, including colleges and seminaries of the Evangelical Lutheran Church in America.

http://www.elca.org/index.html

Here's an example of how one public broadcasting foundation has used its home page as a development tool. It gives member information and takes pledges, although not actual charges to a credit card.

http://www.wgbh.org

These are only a few examples of the spreading use of the Internet by associations and organizations. Many have found that using electronic technology is the best way to disseminate information about their work and services. As shown, once connected to the Internet, you can assess some of the listed guides to help you use it.

The next chapter will give sites for nonprofit research on the Internet.

13

Research Resources on the Internet Nonprofits

*"If anyone thinks that the mesh of a net is an
independent, isolated thing, he is mistaken. It is called a
net because it is made up of a series of interconnected
meshes, and each mesh has its place and responsibility
to other meshes."*

Buddha

Contrary to popular belief and media hype, all informa- tion known to mankind is not on the Internet. As previ- ously mentioned, one estimate, and it can be nothing else, guesses a fraction of one percent of the world's knowledge is there. Reference libraries will not soon, if ever, be closed with everything they contain available only from the computer. You will not soon have to turn on your computer to read the morn- ing newspaper. But you can now — if you want to.

Searching the Internet's World Wide Web takes a great deal of patience, thus the World Wide Wait nickname. Each re- searcher must decide whether the time spent surfing the Inter- net is worth what is retrieved. Many sites get you to company data, but you get only what the company wants to tell. Some- times the information comes straight from the public relations office. After all, this is a capitalistic system and most things of commercial value still require some payment for them.

With that disclaimer, here are some Internet research sites. They were chosen because of their potential usefulness to the nonprofit community. As with the other electronic research tools described in previous chapters, these may offer new ways to find the data most needed in nonprofit offices. The Internet is not the answer to the world's problems, but it is an amazing, somewhat frustrating, communication and research tool.

This list is not intended to be a critical review of the Web sites. Instead, the addresses are listed with just a brief description. It is up to the researcher to determine which are the most useful for his or her nonprofit office. Some work wonderfully well; others may drive you crazy! How patient you will be with each site will depend on how badly you need the information.

Many of these Internet addresses link to other sites. This means while connected to one site, you can click on another listed site and be transferred there. Remember switchboard operators? These links work somewhat the same way without the human factor.

CORPORATE/BUSINESS/FINANCIAL INFORMATION

One of the most useful Internet sites for nonprofit research is the Securities and Exchange Commission's EDGAR (Electronic Data Gathering and Retrieval) system. It provides access to SEC filings on American companies, including the 10-K annual reports, proxy statements (those very useful items — here called DEF14A), and prospectuses.

When funding for experimental Internet access to SEC reports ran out in 1995, the service was in danger of vanishing. Fortunately, the SEC decided to continue the service. Having free information on companies is a boon for nonprofit researchers; such information, as offered by commercial companies, is quite expensive.

http://www.sec.gov

New York University, which helped establish the original free EDGAR project, continues to offer free access using the

EDGAR data from Disclosure Inc. This interface allows easy searching by company name or stock ticker symbol. If you are confused by all those SEC abbreviations and numbers, check out this New York University site that describes what each means.

http://edgar.stern.nyu.edu/general.html

___

Get a daily market summary and information from the American Stock Exchange.

http://www.amex.com

___

The Ranking Library is a compilation of lists of the largest, the most, and the best, compiled by several publications. Included are corporations, colleges, law firms, and the like.

http://wright.mech.utah.edu:555/rank/old.htm

___

Networth Internet Information Center links to more than 500 public company Web sites.

http://networth.galt.com/

http://networth.galt.com/www.home/insider/publico.htm

___

An example of a company that offers research service over the Internet for a fee is Prospex with FRED (Full-Text Retrieval of EDGAR Documents). It searches through corporate proxy statements for indications of wealth. Looking for someone whose company has just gone public? Try the Initial Public Offering documents found here.

http://prospex.com/FRED.html

___

It is hard to keep track of who has merged with whom these days. These Internet sites will help with mergers and acquisitions.

http://www.netresource.com/wsn

http://www.maol.com/maol

———

A very large file on international business is:

http://www.zurich.ibm.com/wwwcomdirectory.html

———

Searching for business leaders in Hong Kong? This will help.

http://farecast.com/hongkong/directory.html

———

European Business Directory is a searchable index to 150,000 corporations in over 25 countries.

http://www.europages.com

———

Japanese firms are listed at this site, with English and Japanese language pages.

http://helios.jicst.go.jp/dir-www/com.html

WDCM BioGopher gives access to Japanese Gopher sites, some that include biographical information on Japanese business persons and information on Asian names.

gopher: fragrans.riken.go.jp

———

This Massachusetts Institute of Technology Web site includes stock charts for hundreds of companies with links to additional financial resources.

http://www.ai.mit.edu/stocks/html

———

QuoteCom Data Service offers a combination of free and for-fee corporate and stock information, including historical quotes. For the fee service you will need a password, but try this to begin.

http://www.quote.com

For further information, e-mail: services@quote.com

Put "help" as subject for automatic response.

———

Do you suspect the company you are researching may have gone bankrupt? Check this site for a list of such companies and other data. There are fees for some information.

http://bankrupt.com/

———

Business and market news is from the *Wall Street Journal* and updated continually throughout the day at this site. It includes news about people making news.

http://update.wsj.com

The *Wall Street Journal* has a Web site that connects to the sites of many companies with which it has some connections, such as its advertisers. The *Journal* publishes an Internet directory periodically.

http://www.adnet.wsj.com for the Internet Directory

The next address gives text of the Personal Technology column from the Thursday *Wall Street Journal*, but back columns are not archived. The column often gives tips for corporate research.

http://ptech.wsj.com

———

Hoover's Handbooks of corporate information can be found at this Web site. It gives a list of 8,000 companies, plus stock quotes, and a pitch for Hoover business titles. It includes a link to corporate home pages and the List of Lists collected from various publications.

http://www.hoovers.com

———

A good place to check if the company you are researching has a Web site is the Virtual Yellow Pages.

http://www.imsworld.com/yp

———

Is your university development office considering establishing a Web site? Take a look at this index to the sites of university alumni and development offices.

http://weber.u.washington.edu/~dev/others.html

BIOGRAPHICAL AND GENEALOGICAL INFORMATION

The Community of Science Web site includes biographical data on over 40,000 individual scientists and researchers in the United States and Canada, with current positions, organizational membership, areas of expertise, patents, publications, and education.

http://best.gdb.org

———

West's Legal Directory (WLD) is on the Internet. It makes it easy to locate information on law firms, government offices, corporate law offices, and lawyers in the United States and Canada. Information on individual lawyers includes basic biographical information.

http://www.westpub.com/WLDInfo/WLD.

———

Determining genealogical connections between donors and prospects is an important function for many development offices. ROOTS-L Resources Pages and Mailing List gives message archives and a file library of useful techniques. See Chapter 11 for the mailing list address, or check this Web site.

http://www.smartlink.net/~leverich/roots-l.html

———

GenServ System (Genealogical Search) includes more than two million names in its data files. It offers one free surname search per e-mail address, then charges $12 annually for full access to the database. Try searching your own surname. The results, with additional information about the service, will come to your e-mail address.

http://soback.kornet.nm.kr/~cmanis

―――――

Another genealogical site is *Everton's Genealogical Helper*, a Web site from the magazine that has long helped family-tree searchers.

http://www.everton.com/index.html

ETHNIC INTERNET RESOURCES

A-Z of Jewish and Israel Related Resources is packed with links to other Internet sites.

http://www.ort.org/anjy/resource/a-z.html

―――――

AfriNET is a World Wide Web site that lists black-oriented sites on the Internet.

http://www.afrinet.net

A similar listing is the Universal Black Pages.

http://ww.gatech.edu/bgsu/blackpages.html

―――――

NetNoir (keyword NETNOIR) is on America Online with special interest for African Americans.

CompuServe's Afro-American Culture and Arts Forum (GO AFRO) is sponsored by *American Visions* magazine.

―――――

Information for the Hispanic community is offered at these sites. The first site is from the Hispanic Association on Corporate Responsibility and has a philanthropic opportunities page. It links to other sites.

http://www.hispanic.org/

Others provide different types of information.

http://www.catalog.com/favision/latnoweb

http://www.clark.net/pub/jgbustam/heritage/heritage.html

http://www.hisp.com/ (This is an online version of *Hispanic Magazine* with links to other Web sites.)

FEDERAL GOVERNMENT AND POLITICAL INFORMATION

FedWorld is the largest government-focused electronic information and communication service in the nation. It is a gateway to government information and offers a freeway to many government agencies. Although not supported with appropriated funds, it is a fully self-supported agency.

So, what's available at this site? First of all, federal jobs information as listed with the Office of Personnel Management. The Catalog of Federal Domestic Assistance (CFDA) can be searched by keyword here. Internet users can use this WWW address to get to FedWorld, then access 140 bulletin boards.

Once into FedWorld, the user can search through government documents using keywords for grant and other information.

http://www.fedworld.gov

———

The Catalog of Federal Domestic Assistance lists all federal government agencies that provide either grant funds or services. The before-mentioned "Grant Getter's Guide to the Internet" contains a link to the CFDA on the Tennessee URL site:

http://gopher.uidaho.edu:70/1s/e-pubs/grant

The CFDA is also available on the CARL database described later.

———

Grants Web is an attempt to organize a large collection of federal grants with information on grantmaking and legal issues. It includes the CFDA and information on many non-federal programs, also.

http://infoserv.rttonet.psu.edu/gweb.htm

———

Grants Net is a network under the U.S. Government's National Performance Review (based in the office of the Vice President). It provides users with access to a wide range of government grants information, including funding opportunities and contact persons.

gopher://gopher.os.dhhs.gov:70/11/Topics/grantsnet

A growing number of important government documents are appearing on the Internet. At no charge, the *Congressional Record*, the *Federal Register*, congressional bills, and other government documents are available with GPO Access.

http://www.access.gpo.gov/su_docs/

Another site for the *Federal Register* is this.

http://www.istech.com/tore-fr.html

If you only knew which of your friends (okay, prospects and donors) gave large amounts to political candidates, it might give you some clue about his or her inclination to make a donation to your organization. You can find out via the Internet in the Federal Election Commission report. It tells who gave and how much.

http://world.std.com/~mcngopher://c-span.org/11/Resource3

U.S. Geographic Survey has a Geographic Names Database that gives the correct spelling and location within which state and county.

gopher://george.peabody.yale.edu:71/1

And the postal ZIP code? It's here at this site.

http://www.usps.gov:80/ncsc/lookup_zip+4.html

Even though you are warned, when you click in, that the data you will receive is four years old, it may be useful to know if the person you are researching owns an airplane. The Federal Aviation Administration lists private airplane owners.

http://www.via.net./test.html

The U.S. Census Bureau provides demographic data at this site.

http://www.census.gov

The government-issued *Occupational Outlook Handbook* can be found at this site. It offers "generic" salary information as well as the future of specific occupations. Here it is provided on the Internet from the University of Missouri-St.Louis.

gopher://umslvma.umsl.edu

At the menu, choose "The Library," then "Government Information."

Library of Congress. The LOCIS (Library of Congress Information System) and LC MARVEL (Library of Congress Machine-Assisted Realization of the Virtual Electronic Library) consist of several accessible sections of interest to nonprofit researchers, including:

• LC CATALOG contains files with records for materials held by the Library of Congress as well as other agencies and research institutions.

• Federal Legislation contains summaries, abstracts, status information, and histories of congressional bills and resolutions.

• Copyright contains records for all materials copyrighted since 1978.

http://www.loc.gov

gopher://marvel.loc.gov/

For U.S. congressional information, for both the House and the Senate, Internet access with graphics appeared in early 1995. It includes the full text of recently introduced bills and their status. Named for Thomas Jefferson, his face appears when you click on.

> http://thomas.loc.gov

Congressional Black Caucus Information

> http://drum.ncsc.org/~carter/CBC.html

White House. Besides information about what is going on there, this site gives information on executive branch agencies and publications available to the public. (The creators of this system had some fun. The site includes a snapshot of first cat, Socks.)

> http://www.whitehouse.gov

The Internal Revenue Service. I've heard you can download certain federal income tax forms here. Very useful on April 14, but do not wait until then. The site may be very crowded.

> http://www.ustreas.gov/treasury/bureaus/irs.html

Both the Democrats and the Republicans can be reached online. Tell party officials for both parties what you think.

Democratic National Committee

> http://www.democrats.org/

GOP Online

> http://www.gop.org/

GENERAL REFERENCE

Britannica Online comes from the editors of the *Encyclopedia Britannica* and is useful for serious research, as is its parent, the print encyclopedia. This is a fee-based service that can provide excellent reference help. The *Encyclopedia Britannica* lagged behind other encyclopedia companies in providing a digitized version, but now it is the first to offer a complete 44-million-word edition via the Internet. It gets good reviews. For prices and other details, send e-mail to sales.eb.com. Or check this site:

> http://www.eb.com

This might be sort of fun. To find out who is celebrating a birthday today, or any day, check this WWW address from the *Encyclopedia Britannica*. Surprise someone with a birthday card.

> http://www.eb.com/calendar/calendar.html

The Knight-Ridder Information DIALOG system has a home page on the Internet to disseminate information on their products and services. Users can register for service directly from the home page. Those who understand how DIALOG works will welcome quick access to Bluesheets, the essential search tools to be studied for best database searching success. They are available on the home page. At this site, you can sign up for an automatic listserv mailing from DIALOG, read the *Chronolog* newsletter, or read the FAQs at this address.

> http://www.dialog.com

For general reference help from dictionaries and thesauruses, try this one.

> http://www.cs.cmu.edu/Web/references.html

Are you ever stumped by an acronym? The University of Wisconsin has put up a list of acronyms and what they stand for.

> http://maggie.cs.wisc.edu:1234/misc.acronyms

All kinds of tourist information or just information about a particular city, state, or country can be found at these Virtual Tourist sites.

Virtual Tourist - http://wings.buffalo.edu/world/

Virtual Tourist 2 - http://wings.buffalo.edu/world/vt2

Going on a trip overseas? Check this out for current exchange rates.

http://gnn.com/cgi-bin/gnn/currency

The Internet can become your own travel agent. The Internet Travel Network gives free flight information and prices. It offers access to the Apollo reservation system to let you check flight availability and look for the best prices. Once you find what you are looking for, it can send your itinerary to a local agent for ticketing.

http://www.itn.net/itn

Or do you want to check the weather at your U.S. travel destination? Try these, or try the Web site from your local television station's weather room.

http://www.nj.com

http://www.princeton.edu/Webweather/ww.html

Add a four-day forecast for cities around the world, with this.

http://www.intellicast.com/index/html

LIBRARY ONLINE CATALOGS

HARVARD hollis.harvard.edu

LIBRARY OF CONGRESS http://www.loc.gov (for access to more than 26 million entries)

NEW YORK PUBLIC LIBRARY nyplgate.nypl.org (log-in as nypl for access to all materials acquired since 1971.)

UNIVERSITY OF VIRGINIA gopher.lib.virginia.edu

telnet: ublan.acc.virginia.edu

Colorado Alliance of Libraries (CARL) telnet: database. carl.org

Free access to many library catalogs is now part of that system.

NEWSPAPERS, PLUS MAGAZINE AND NEWSPAPER INDEXES

Many newspapers now maintain Web sites. Some allow full-text searching and some just give information about the newspaper. The best advice is to check the sites for those papers that interest you and see what is available. Keep in mind, this type of research is growing daily. What isn't available today may be tomorrow.

———

UnCover is an indexing service to periodical tables of content from the Colorado Alliance of Libraries (CARL). Searching the UnCover database is free, but for other UnCover services you will need an account. Sometimes your library has direct gateway access, but you need to set up an account for fax delivery of articles to you. Users can set up a deposit account for $100 or pay by credit card.

UnCover is one of those electronic services that would have been impossible a short ten years ago. It's quite amazing. Individuals can access the contents of about 20,000 journals, then request copies online for $8.50 per article, plus a copyright royalty fee. (With UnCover Single Order Source, users can order articles by fax, e-mail, or telephone, without searching for them online. The charge is $10 per article, and the order is confirmed within two hours.)

UnCover's almost 20,000 periodical titles, dating back to 1989, include about 51 percent scientific and technology journals, about 40 percent social science titles (including many business-related titles), and about 9 percent arts and humanities titles.

Perhaps best of all, for an annual fee of $20, individuals can set up a profile request with UnCover for an e-mail copy of the tables of content of up to fifty journal titles, sent to you just after publication. You can also set up a search strategy to be run each week, looking for hits on your topics. Or you can search by name, which will pick up that name as author or subject of an article. Very useful in prospect or donor research.

Once you have the citation, if you wish, you can order copies of individual articles. For information and application material by fax, call 1-800-787-7979 or 1-303-758.3030.

You can reach UnCover with the following Internet addresses.

Telnet to: database.carl.org

UnCover's home page is at:

http://www.carl.org/uncover/unchome.html

———

Some newspapers have their own e-mail address or a Web site. Here's one for the *Washington Post* with full text of the current week of that newspaper.

http://americast.com/PUBS/HP/wpost/menu.html

———

Abstracts to articles in leading newspapers are from Carnegie Mellon University Libraries Front Door site. A who's who section is a directory of that university's faculty, staff, and students.

http://www.library.cmu.edu/News/950.html

———

American Demographics and the companion *Marketing Tools* magazines are available online. You can read the current issue and others going back about six months. It allows keyword searching of articles.

http://www.marketingtools.com

———

The Newslink site links to more than 1,800 newspapers, magazine, broadcast companies, and other electronic publishing sources. It can be used to search for news items on prospects.

http://www.newslink.org/

The *Minneapolis Star Tribune* promises complete archives to articles back to 1986 with no cost to read and 50 cents to download an article. At a subscription rate of $5 per month, it includes information about the Twin Cities area.

http://www.startribune.com.

To get information on searching the *Wall Street Journal* and the related Dow Jones News Service, Global Business Reports and Press Release Wire, try this site. Searching is not free, but you can see what is available for a fee.

http://dowvision.wais.net/

The LEXIS/NEXIS Web site is listed below. Sorry, it's not free access to the whole database. You may save on telecommunications charges, but regular charges apply. This site lists sources available in the service with subscription information.

http://www.lexis-nexis.com

The *New York Times* has an eight-page fax digest. Find it at this Web site.

http://www.nytimesfax.com

Several newspapers and magazines publish electronic editions over the Internet, including the *San Francisco Chronicle and Examiner*, the *San Jose Mercury News, Tacoma News Tribune,* and others. These and other sources can be found through Yahoo at this address.

http://www.yahoo.com/News/

To search the *San Francisco Examiner* and the San *Francisco Chronicle*, use this site.

http://www.sfgate.com/search/

To search the *Palo Alto Weekly*:

http://www.service.com/PAW/morgue/home.html

An online version of one of the country's most popular newspapers, *USA Today*, offers quick national and international news, current events, weather forecasts, and, of course, sports.

http://www.usatoday.com/

The *San Diego Daily Transcript* offers a virtual financial reference section about that southern California area.

http://www.sddt.com/

Time Warner Publications have a connection to the Internet and provides full-text searching. Included are *Time, Fortune, People,* and *Sports Illustrated.*

http://pathfinder.com

For British and international news, this site posts each day's top story and the news in brief the world over.

http://www.ft.com/

http://www.usa.ft.com

NONPROFIT PUBLICATIONS ONLINE

American Philanthropy Review is the first electronic subscription magazine devoted to American philanthropy and the nonprofit sector.

http://www205.198.215.242/

Chronicle of Philanthropy provides a summary of the current issue every other Tuesday. It also lists conferences, workshops, and other events by region and grant deadlines.

Send an e-mail message to: listproc@nonprofit.com

Message: Subscribe Chronicle firstname lastname organization

The _Internet Prospector_ is a monthly electronic publication that comes automatically to subscribers to the e-mail listserv PRSPCT-L. It began in November 1994.

See Chapter 11 for PRSPCT-L subscription instructions. When you subscribe you will get FAQs about the service.

One way to get back issues of the _Internet Prospector_ is with a link from the MacArthur Foundation home page's "hot links" section at

http://www.macfdn.org/

That links to this site:

http://plains.uwyo.edu/~prospect/archives.html

The _Non-Profit Times_ has an Internet site for users to read about current topics affecting the nonprofit world.

http://haven.ios.com/~nptimes/index.html

Philanthropic Studies Index from Indiana University and Purdue University's Payton Philanthropic Studies Library is a reference to literature on all aspects of fund raising and management of nonprofit organizations.

http://www-Lib.iupui.edu/philanthropy/psl.html

Philanthropy Journal

This Web site, maintained by the _News and Observer_ in Raleigh, North Carolina, includes abstracts from issues of that publication.

http://www.nando.net/philant/philant.html

The Foundation Center's *Philanthropy News Digest* picks up news relating to that subject from newswires and newspapers. It is available on the Center's home page.

http://fdncenter.org/phil.philmain.html

Planned Giving Today can be read online.

http://www.new3.com/purplecat/pgt/

PUBLIC RECORDS FROM STATES

Internet Prospector volunteers cruised the Internet to find Web sites for online incorporation records. The state-by-state list was a part of the November 1995 issue. Find it at this site.

http://plains.uwyo.edu/~prospect/archives.html

REAL ESTATE

Nonprofit researchers often need property values and other real estate information. Several sites are listed in the "Internet Real Estate Directory" at this location.

http://www.onramp.net:80/ired/relistint.html

The National Association of Realtors (NAR) unveiled a service in November 1995 that will permit anyone with an Internet connection to comb through data contained in local Multiple Listing Services of houses for sale, regardless of where the searcher lives. It gives a description of the house, its price, and the listing agent. It won't allow the searcher to make direct contact with the seller. After all, it's a tool for the agent; not a "for sale by owner" option.

http://www.realtor.com

HomeNet provides Web addresses for New York City (and some surrounding communities) commercial property rentals with descriptions and prices. It gives average sales prices for properties in many of those locations.

> http://www.netprop.com/

HomeWeb, begun in August 1995, included over 60,000 real estate listings by mid-November of that year. More listings are promised.

> http://www.us-digital.com/homeweb

You can find real estate listings for several areas from Bay-Net in San Francisco.

> http://www.baynet.com

Or do you prefer Wisconsin? This database is also a part of Microsoft Network, accessed by clicking an icon there.

> http://realdirect.com

Check with realty companies for similar Web sites in your city.

TELEPHONE AND ZIP-CODE DIRECTORY ASSISTANCE

Sure enough, telephone number information at 411 has shown up on the Internet. A California company, PC411, continually updates a database of phone numbers, addresses, and ZIP codes of more than 95 million residences and businesses. Instead of calling 411, download the PC411 software from the company's Web page. That costs $15, which includes a $15 usage credit. To search, hit the find button. PC411 dials into the company database. The charge is 50 cents for local calls (about what your local 411 charges), but you will save on long-distance directory assistance.

http://www.pc411.com

———

This site lets you search for area codes using the 3-digit prefix to find what city or state includes that phone number.

http://www.natltele.com/form.html

———

You can browse the directory of AT&T 800 numbers or search by keyword or 800 phone number.

http://att.net/dir800

———

Or look for a ZIP code if you have a partial address. Besides the previously mentioned site listed in the Federal Government section, this will give you ZIP+4 codes.

http://www.cedar.buffalo.edu/adserv.html

———

Access to more than 95 million U.S. phone numbers and addresses is possible from SearchAmerica. There is a credit card charge for queries.

http://www.searchamerica.com

E-MAIL ADDRESSES

One option for finding an individual's e-mail address is called Four11. It claims over a million listings of individuals with their e-mail addresses gleaned from various sources, primarily bulletin boards. You can search it free, as long as you agree to enter your own name and e-mail address. Fair enough.

http://www.Four11.com

———

Or, try LookUp. You don't have to register, but they hope you will.

http://www.lookup.com/

———

The Internet White Pages links to directories of e-mail addresses, domain names, and organization names.

http://home.netscape.com/home/internet-white-pages.html

CAREERS AND JOB OPPORTUNITIES

For jobs in nonprofit organizations, see the listing of listservs in Chapter 11. Many include announcements for positions available for persons working in the area covered by the mailing list. For example, APRA has a job board at

http://weber.u.washington.edu/~dlamb/apra/APRA.html

Looking for a job in the Federal Government? This lists current openings for viewing and downloading.

http://www.fedworld.gov

Or, telnet to: fedworld.gov

The Council for Advancement and Support of Education (CASE) offers its popular job announcements on its home page. Jobs in education, fund raising, alumni and public relations, communications, and student recruitment are listed. Best of all, the openings can be searched by city or state, job title, or name of institution.

http://www.case.org

gopher to: gopher.case.org

CareerPath.com is a location on the World Wide Web for recruitment advertising. Five large-city newspapers (*The Boston Globe, Chicago Tribune, Los Angeles Times, The New York Times, San Jose Mercury News,* and the *Washington Post*) have combined forces to display their job classified ads on the Internet. To search, pick the newspaper you wish to use, than choose a career category, such as fund raising.

http://www.careerpath.com

———

Both America Online and CompuServe have job opportunities posted as part of their nonprofit forums.

America Online has "access.point" for nonprofit organizations in its Clubs & Interests section. Follow the instructions from screen to screen until you come to the icon listing career/job opportunities. Many job listings are excerpted from "Community Jobs: The National Employment Newspaper for the Non-Profit Sector." Call 1-212-475-1001.

The America Online site offers the "Occupational Profiles Database" with 250 job descriptions from the *Occupational Outlook Handbook*. The keyword to get there is CAREER, then select the icon.

CompuServe (GO CAREERS) leads to a career management forum, but the E-Span Job Search (GO ESPAN) is a way to post a resume to corporations or organizations that pay to advertise online.

AND—EVEN THE BIBLE

The Good Book has been in hotel rooms the world over for decades. Now it's on the Net. You can search passages from five versions in seven languages. Seeing how the verse reads in each version may shed light on its meaning.

http://www.gospelcom.net/bible

Epilogue

Technology's effect on the entire prospect research and fund-raising process may be dramatic, but it will never take the place of human interaction. As technology develops beyond what it is today, the temptation may be to think of the researched prospect or donor only as some kind of technologically possible pursuit and to forget the human element.

People helping others is the reason behind philanthropy. It is also the spirit behind the reason for most nonprofit organizations. Technology is one element, but not even the most important one. The end result of the electronic research, and how it improves the organization's mission, is what matters.

If I have learned anything from writing this book, it is that technology moves quickly. What was not true one month became true the next. I suspect that, in the next six months, things will develop just as fast. No one, not even Microsoft's Bill Gates, is quite sure where this computerization, which he has been so involved in developing, will take us.

It is certain that more and more information will become available on an electronic resource. Now, most reference items have a print equivalent. That will probably change as more reference tools are published only electronically.

Who knows where the Internet is taking us? It is exciting, though a bit overwhelming, to watch. For certain, every day new items are being added to the Internet. It is estimated every few seconds another home page is established. Some just clutter cyperspace; others are spectacular and very useful. Those home pages will become more user friendly as web creators are more experienced and publishers realize this potential for information transmission.

What needs to happen, and it probably will, is that some information we now pay dearly for will become available for the taking—even in this capitalistic system. Other data will be available only to those who have paid an access fee and received a password. For example, many scholarly journals are now published on the Internet rather than in small numbers on paper, sent to a few university subscribers. On the Internet, even for a subscription fee, more scholars could find the needed article and download it. Will that make information more, or less, accessible? Time will tell.

Although the nonprofit world was behind the business world in the use of electronics for research, they are catching up quickly. I hope the information in this book will open the way for further investigation to the wonders of what is available electronically. The best advice I can give to readers is to explore the possibilities.

As the electronic information world grows, what worries me, as I finish this book, is that the next edition should be started tomorrow.

Addresses

ABI/INFORM - UMI
620 South Third Street
Louisville, KY 40202-2475
1-800-626-2823

AfroLink Software
1815 Wellington Road
Los Angeles, CA 90019-5945

America Business Information
5711 South 86th Circle
P.O. Box 27347
Omaha, NE 68127
   1-800-555-5666
   1-402-593-4600
   1-402-592-9000 (For Online
Service)

America Online
8619 Westwood Center Drive
Vienna, VA 22182-2285
   1-800-827-6364
   1-703-448-8700

American Medical Association
515 N. State Street
Chicago, IL 60610
   1-312-645-5000

AT&T Business Network
P.O.5025
Bristol, CT 06011-9944
   1-800-224-7505
   1-800-665-4492

Banner Blue - Family Tree
Broderbund Software
P.O. Box 6125

Novato, CA 94948
   1-800-521-6263

BASELINE II Inc.
838 Broadway, 4th Floor
New York, NY 10003
   1-800-242-7546
   1-212-254-8235

BiblioData
P.O. Box 61
Needham Heights, MA 02194
   1-617-444-1154

BizBooks, Inc.
First Citizens Plaza
128 S. Tryon Street, Suite 2200
Charlotte, NC 28202
   1-800-486-3289

Bloomberg Financial Markets
Bloomberg Business News
499 Park Avenue
New York, NY 10022
   1-212-318-2000

BRS and BRS/AfterDark
8000 Westpark Drive
McLean, VA 22102
   1-800-289-4277

BUSINESS WIRE
44 Montgomery Street, 39th Floor
San Francisco, CA 94104
   1-415-986-4422

CACI Marketing Systems
1100 North Glebe Road
Arlington, VA 22201

1-800-292-2224 (East Coast Office)
1-800-394-3690 (West Coast Office)

CARL Corporation
3801 E. Florida Avenue, Suite 300
Denver, CO 80210
1-303-758-3030

CD Light
8861 S.Silverstone Way
Sandy, UT 84093-1679
1-800-571-3914

CDA/Investnet
3265 Meridian Parkway, Suite 130
Ft.Lauderdale, FL 33331
1-800-933-4446
1-305-384-1500

CDA Investment Technologies
1355 Piccard Drive
Rockville, MD 20850
1-301-975-9600

CDB Infotek
Six Hutton Centre
Santa Ana, CA 92707
1-800-427-3747

Chronicle of Philanthropy
1255 23rd Street NW, Suite 775
Washington, DC 20037
1-800-287-6072
1-202-466-1200

CompuServe Information Service
5000 Arlington Center Boulevard
P.O. Box20212
Columbus, OH 43220
1-800-848-8990
1-800-487-9197

Consumer Reports Home Price Service
Consumers Union
101 Truman Ave.
Yonkers, NY 10703-1057
1-800-775-1212
1-914-378-2000

Contacts Influential Division
American Business Marketing
510 First Avenue North, Suite 303
Minneapolis, MN 55403
1-612-672-9974

Corel Order Center
P.O. Box 3595
Salinas, CA 93912
1-800-836-3729

D&B Marketplace Information Corporation
460 Totten Pond Road
Walthan, MA 02154-1906
1-800-505-3237
1-800-590-0065

DAMAR Real Estate Information Service
3610 Central Avenue
Riverside, CA 92506
1-800-345-7334

Database Technologies, Inc.
100 East Sample Road, Ste. 200
Pompano Beach, Florida
1-800-279-7710
1-305-781-5221

DataQuick Information Systems
9171 Towne Centre Drive, 6th Floor
San Diego, CA 92122
1-800-863-INFO
1-619-455-6900

Where the Information Is

DataTimes
Parkway Plaza, Suite 450
14000 Quail Springs Parkway
Oklahoma City, OK 73134
  1-800-642-2525
  1-405-751-6400

DeLorme Mapping Company
P.O. Box 298
Freeport, ME 04032
  1-800-452-5931
  1-207-865-9291

DIALOG Information Services
3460 Hillview Avenue
Palo Alto, CA 94303-0993
  1-800-334-2564
  1-415-858-3785

Digital Directory Assistance, Inc.
PhoneDisc USA
6931 Arlington Road, Suite 405
Bethesda, MD 20814
  1-800-284-8353
  1-301-657-8548

Disclosure Incorporated
5161 River Road
Bethesda, MD 20816
  1-800-843-7747
  1-800-846-0365
  1-301-951-1300

Disclosure - SEC On-Line, Inc.
201 Moreland Road, Suite 2
Hauppauge, NY 11788
  1-516-864-7200

DoNet
Alexander O'Neill Haas &
  Martin, Inc.
181 Fourteenth St. NE, Suite 500
Atlanta, GA 30309
  1-800-490-8039
  1-404-875-7575

Dow Jones Business Information
  Services
P.O. Box 300
Princeton, NJ 08543-0300
  1-800-815-5100
  1-609-520-4664

Dun's Million Dollar Disc
Three Sylvan Way
Parsippany, NJ 07054-3896
  1-800-255-9220
  1-201-605-6000

Forbes Inc.
60 Fifth Avenue
New York, NY 10011
  1-212-620-2200

Foundation Center
79 Fifth Avenue
New York, NY 10003-3076
  1-800-424-9836
  1-212-620-4230

Gale Research Inc.
835 Penobscot Bldg.
Detroit, MI 48226-4094
  1-800-877-GALE
  1-313-961-2242

Genie Information Services
401 North Washington Street
Rockville, MD 20849-6403
  1-800-638-9636
  1-301-340-4000

Hoover's Guides
The Reference Press, Inc.
6448 Hwy 290 East, Suite E104
Austin, TX 78723-9823
  1-800-486-8666
  1-512-454-7778

IDI Magic Valley Technologies
Corporation
Fedral Money Retriever
315 Falls Avenue
P.O. Box 2301
Twin Falls, ID 83303-2301
1-800-804-5270
1-208-734-5663

InfoEd, Inc.
SPIN: Sponsored Programs
Information Network
453 New Karner Road
Albany, NY 12205
1-800-727-6427
1-518-464-0691

Information Access Company
362 Lakeside Drive
Foster City, CA 94404
1-800-227-8431
1-415-378-5200

Information America
One Georgia Center
600 West Peachtree Street NW,
Suite 1200
Atlanta, GA 30308
1-800-235-4008
1-404-892-1800

Information Today, Inc.
143 Old Marlton Pike
Medford, NJ 08055-8750
1-609-654-6266

Knight-Ridder Information, Inc.
2440 El Camino Real
Mountain View, CA 94040
1-800-3DIALOG
1-415-258-8800

LEXIS-NEXIS
Mead Data Central, Inc.
9443 Springboro Pike

P.O. Box 933
Dayton, OH 45401
1-800-227-4908

Lusk/TRW REDI Real Estate
Information Service
1100 Bonifant Street
Silver Spring, MD 20910
1-800-345-REDI
1-301-588-6700

MapLink Corporation
5720 LBJ Freeway, Suite 180
Dallas, TX 75240-6328
1-800-352-3414
1-214-231-1400

Marquis Who's Who
Reed Reference Publishing
121 Chanlon Road
New Providence, NJ 07974
1-800-323-3288
1-908-771-8711

Martindale-Hubbell, Inc.
Reed Reference Publishing
121 Chanlon Road
New Providence, NJ 07974
1-800-323-3288
1-908-464-6800

Mead Data Central, Inc.
LEXIS-NEXIS
9443 Springboro Pike
Dayton, OH 45401-0933
1-800-227-4908
1-513-859-1608
1-800-843-6476
(NEXISExpress)

Mecklermedia
20 Ketchum Street
Westport, CT 06880
1-203-226-6967

Metromail
R.R. Donnelley & Sons Company
Regional Offices - Call for Info
   1-800-793-2536
   1-800-228-4571 (For Search
Service)

Microsoft Corporation
One Microsoft Way
Redmond, WA 98052-6394
   1-800-426-9400
   1-800-386-5550 (Microsoft
Network)

Moody's Investors Service
99 Church Street
New York, NY 10007
   1-800-342-5647 ext. 0546

National Association of Realtors
430 N. Michigan Ave.
Chicago, IL 60611-4087
   1-312-329-8200

National Resources Services
6748 East 26 Court
Tulsa, OK 74129
   1-918-836-2054

New York Times Online Services
520 Speedwell Avenue
Morris Plain, NJ 07950
   1-201-829-0036

NewsBank
58 Pine Street
New Canaan, CT 06840-5426
   1-800-762-8182
   1-203-966-5906

NewsNet
945 Haverford Road
Bryn Mawr, PA 19010
   1-800-952-0122
   1-610-527-8030

OCLC Online Computer Library
Center, Inc.
6565 Frantz Road
Dublin, OH 43017
   1-800-848-5878
   1-614-764-6000

Orca Knowledge Systems
P.O. Box 280
San Anselmo, CA 94979
   1-800-868-ORCA
   1-415-382-8635

Oryx Press
4041 North Central Ave., Suite 700
Phoenix, AZ 85012-3397
   1-800-279-6799
   1-602-265-2651

PC-411
9800 LaCienega Blvd., Suite 411
Inglewood, CA 90301
   1-800-2GET-411
   1-310-645-1114

Pemberton Press Inc.
462 Danbury Road
Wilton, CT 06897-2126
   1-800-248-8466

PR Newswire, Inc.
806 Plaza Three
Jersey City, NJ 07311-3801
   1-800-832-5522

Prodigy Services Company
445 Hamilton Avenue
White Plains, NY 10601
   1-800-776-3449
   1-914-448-8000

Profound Inc.
655 Madison Avenue
New York, NY 10021
   1-800-435-7560
   1-800-638-7139

1-212-750-6900

ProPhone - Pro CD Inc.
222 Rosewood Drive
Danvers, MA 01923-4520
1-800-992-3766
1-508-750-0055

Prospex Inc.
300 Westage Business Center,
Ste. 390
P.O. Box 517
Fishkill, NY 12524
1-914-897-3111

Reed Reference Publishing
121 Chanlon Road
New Providence, NJ 07974
1-800-621-9669
1-800-521-8110

Reference Press, Inc.
6448 Highway 290 E, Suite E-104
Austin, TX 78723
1-512-454-7778

Research Grant Guides, Inc.
12798 West Forest Hill Blvd.,
Suite 304
West Palm Beach, FL 33414
1-407-795-6129

SoftLine Information Inc.
Ethnic NewsWatch
65 Broad Street
P.O. Box 16845
Stamford, CT 06901
1-800-524-7922
1-203-968-8878

Standard & Poor's
25 Broadway
New York, NY 10004
1-800-233-2310
1-212-208-8786

Staff Directories, Ltd.
P.O. Box 62
Mount Vernon, VA 22121-0062
1-703-739-0900

Taft Group
835 Penobscot Bldg.
645 Griswold Street
Detroit, MI 48226
1-800-877-8238

Time, Inc.
Time-Life Bldg.
New York, NY 10020
1-212-333-4066

TRW/REDI Property Data
3610 Central Avenue
Riverside, CA 92506
1-800-345-7334

UMI - ProQuest
300 North Zeeb Road
Ann Arbor, MI 48106-1346
1-800-521-0600
1-313-761-4700
1-415-433-5500

UMI Online Services
620 South 3rd Street
Louisville, KY 40202-2297
1-800-626-2823

UnCover Company
3801 E. Florida Av., Suite 200
Denver, CO 80210
1-303-758-3030

U.S. General Services
  Administration
Federal Domestic Assistance
  Catalog Staff
Reporters Building, RM 101
300 Seventh Street, SW
Washington, DC 20407
1-202-708-5126

Where the Information Is

USWest Search Disc
3190 South Vaughn Way, 2nd
    Floor North
Aurora, CO 80014-3506
    1-800-431-6600

Walker's Manual of Western
    Corporations
1650 Borel Place, Suite 130
San Mateo, CA 94402
    1-800-258-5737
    1-415-341-1110

Waltman Associates
Century Plaza
1111 3rd Avenue South, Suite 144
Minneapolis, MN 55404
    1-612-338-0772

West Publishing
620 Opperman Drive
Eagan, MN 55123
    1-800-328-9352
    1-612-687-7000

H.W. Wilson
950 University Avenue
Bronx, NY 10452
    1-800-367-6770
    1-718-588-8400

Zipp Zapp
True Basic
12 Commerce Avenue
West Lebanon, NH 03784
    1-800-436-2111
    1-603-298-8517

Electronic Research Resources: Where to Get Help

Each day new resources are added to the electronic information superhighway. Soon after this book goes to press there will be new products and Web sites that should have been mentioned — if only I had known about them.

Listed below are resources that will help keep researchers in nonprofit organziations informed about new electronic products as they become available.

BOOKS AND PERIODICALS

Advancing Philanthropy: The Journal of NSFRE. National Society of Fund Raising Executives, 1101 King Street, Suite 700, Alexandria, VA 22314. 1-800-666-FUND or 1-703-684-0410.

This quarterly publication comes with membership in the NSFRE. It includes articles and information on current trends, including technology.

American Demographics Magazine. American Demographics, Inc., P.O. 68, Ethic, NY 14851. 1-800-828-1133. $60 per year for twelve monthly issues.

Studying the demographic structure and trends of a specific area has become an important part of nonprofit research.

Bergan, Helen J. *Where the Money Is: A Fund Raiser's Guide to the Rich,* 2nd ed., 1992. ISBN: 0-9615277-6-5. BioGuide Press, P.O. 16072, Alexandria, VA 22302. 1-703-820-9045. $29.95 ($2 shipping.)

> Called the "definitive guide" to prospect and donor research for nonprofit organizations. Tells where to find information on individuals and corporations that may lead to a large contribution.

Berkman, Robert I. *Find It Online!* 1994. Windcrest/McGraw-Hill, New York. ISBN 0-8306-4570-5. $19.95.

> The maze of online computer services is described in this book for the casual researcher.

Business Journal Book of Lists. BizBooks, Inc., First Citizens Plaza, 128 S.Tryon Street, Suite 2200, Charlotte, NC 28202. 1-800-486-3289. Price varies.

> Listings of businesses in several categories by geographic region are published in this chain of business newspapers then reprinted in hard copy or on diskette.

CASE Currents. Council for Advancement and Support of Education, 11 Dupont Circle, Suite 400, Washington, DC 20036. 1-202- 328-5900. $95 for annual subscription.

> All aspects of advancement in educational institutions are included in this monthly journal.

The Chronicle of Philanthropy. This "Newspaper of the Non-Profit World" is published biweekly. It includes a Technology column giving details on new products and services. Discussion forums and bulletin boards on the Internet are explained as they become available. The *Chronicle* offers a free preview of the newspaper's next issue, plus an update on forthcoming events in the nonprofit world. Send the following e-mail message to

> chronicle-request@nonprofit.com

subscribe chronicle (your name and organization)

It works not only on the Internet, but with America Online, CompuServe, Prodigy, and most commercial e-mail services.

Subscriptions to the newspaper are $67.50 for one year (24 issues) or $36 for six months (12 issues) from The Chronicle of Philanthropy, P.O. 1989, Marion, OH 43306-2089. Editorial offices are at 1255 23rd Street NW, Suite 775, Washington, DC, 20037. 1-202-466-1200.

Connections. Association of Professional Researchers for Advancement, 414 Plaza Drive, Suite 209, Westmont, IL. 60559. 1-708-655-0177.

Comes with APRA membership and includes new research techniques, Internet sites, and other resources.

Contributions. The "How-to" Source for Nonprofit Professionals. P.O. Box 336, Medfield, MA 02052-0336. 1-508-359-0019. $28 per year for six issues.

Practical columns that cover many aspects of nonprofit management, fund raising, prospect research, board relations, major gifts, demographics, planned giving, and direct mail.

DIALOG User Manual and Thesaurus, New Revised Edition. Foundation Center, 79 Fifth Avenue, New York, NY 10003-3076. 1-800-424-9836. ISBN 0-87954-595-X. $50.

For those using DIALOG to find foundation and corporate grants, this guide gives subject terms and shows how to retrieve facts for online fundraising research.

Directory of Computer and High Technology Grants, 2nd. ed. ISBN 0-945078-07-2. Research Grant Guides, Inc., 12798 West Forest Hill Boulevard, Suite 304, West Palm Beach, FL 33414. 1-407-795-6129. $52.50.

This guide tells where to get financial help to upgrade your computer systems. Includes over 3,000 funding entries. Other directories from this publisher cover grants for specific types of nonprofits. They include articles by Andrew J.Grant on seeking grants using the Internet.

Directory of Public Libraries Offering Information and Referral Services. American Library Association, ALA Order Department, 155 North Wacker Drive, Chicago, IL 60606-1710. 1-800-545-2433, Ext. 7. $28.

Nonprofit researchers may benefit from using local libraries for some of their information needs. This lists more than 200 libraries offering such services. Some are free; others charge fees.

Forbes. Forbes, P.O. Box 10048, DesMoines, IA 50309. 1-800-888-9896. $57 per year for 27 issues.

Forbes includes the annual "400 Wealthiest Americans" in October. Subscription also brings *Forbes ASAP,* a supplement on the information age.

Fortune. Time Customer Service, P.O. Box 60001, Tampa, FL 33660-0001. 1-800-621-8000. $57 per year for 26 issues.

Includes several useful listing of top corporations and wealthy individuals.

Fulltext Sources Online. BiblioData, P.O. Box 61, Needham Heights, MA 02194. 1-617-444-1154. Single January annual issue, $105; January and July issues, $180.

Lists over 5,000 journals, magazines, newspapers, newsletters, and newswires found online in fulltext. Helps you search in the right database to save time and money by knowing coverage dates.

Fund Raising Management. Hoke Communications, Inc., 224 Seventh Street, Garden City, NY 11530. 1-516-746-6700. $54 per year.

Includes articles on electronic use by nonprofit organizations as part of the fundraising process.

Gale Directory of Databases, edited by Kathleen Lopez Nolan. Gale Research Inc., P.O. Box 33477, Detroit, MI 1-800-877-GALE. ISBN 0-8103-8805-7. $215.

Looking for a database on an obscure topic? Check this guide.It lists thousands of databases and tells how to access them.

Godin, Seth. *E-Mail Addresses of the Rich and Famous.* Addison-Wesley, $7.95.

Probably not as useful as it sounds, but it is sort of interesting. Many e-mail addresses may have changed since this was written.

Higley, Stephen Richard. *Privilege, Power and Place: The Geography of the American Upper Class.* Rowman Publishing. 1995. $52 or $21.95, paperback.

An analysis of the 1988 *Social Register* by an urban geographer. It shows where the wealthy live. Most in that register live in New York.

Hoffman, Paul E. *Netscape and World Wide Web for Dummies.* IDG Books. 1995. $19.95.

This friendly guide to the Internet and the World Wide Web will answer many questions for beginners. It lists interesting Web sites.

infoActive: The Telecommunications Monthly for Nonprofits is published by the Center for Media Education, 1511 K Street NW, Suite 518, Washington, DC 20005. 1-202-628-2620. Subscriptions are $35 for a year (ten issues) for individuals, nonprofits, and government institutions and $100 for corporations and other for-profit firms.

This very practical newsletter promotes new technology

for use by nonprofits and strives to make sure that national policy keeps access possible for all.

John, Nancy R. and Edward J. Valauskas. *The Internet Troubleshooter: Help for the Logged-On and Lost.* American Library Association, Chicago. 1-800-545-2433. ISBN: 0-8389-0633-8. $27.00.

This covers real-life problems that can happen on the Internet. It helps a user to connect and to solve problems once online.

Krol, Ed. *The Whole Internet: User's Guide and Catalog.* 2nd ed. 1994. O'Reilly & Associates, 103 Morris Street, Sebastopol, CA 95472. 1-800-998-9938 or 1-707-829-0515. ISBN: 1-56592-063-5. $24.95.

This, perhaps, tells more than you need to know about using the Internet. It includes many Internet features before the World Wide Web became the system of choice.

Levine, John R. and Carol Baroudi. *The Internet for Dummies.* IDG Books, San Mateo, CA 94402. 1993. ISBN: 1-56884-024-1. $19.95.

The title says it all. It is entertaining reading that packs some useful information. The Internet has become more user-friendly since this was written.

Link-Up: The Magazine for Users of Online Services and CD-ROM in Business, Education and at Home. Information Today, Inc., 143 Old Marlton Pike, Medford, NJ 08055-8750. 1-609-654-6266. $27.95 per year for six issues.

Includes up-to-date news on most of the topics covered in this book: online services, CD-ROMs, bulletin boards, and databases.

Magid, Lawrence J. *Cruising Online: Larry Magid's Guide to the New Digital Highways.* Random House, NY. 1994. ISBN 0-679-75155-6. $25.

Goes into detail about the commercial online services (CompuServe, America Online, and Prodigy) with tips for searching each for the general reader.

NEDRA News. New England Development Research Association, 1770 Massachusetts Avenue, Box 288, Cambridge, MA 022140. FAX: 1-617-496-3919.

Included with NEDRA membership. It includes software and technology reviews and tips.

Newspapers Online. 1995. BiblioData, P.O. 61, Needham Heights, MA 02194, 1-617-444-1154. $99.

Includes information on 200 daily North American and international newspapers that are available online in full text.

NonProfit Times. 190 Tamarack Circle, Skillman, NJ 08558. 1-609-1251. $59 per year for twelve issues.

Included with articles on nonprofit management are articles dealing with technology.

Nonprofit World: The National Nonprofit Leadership and Management Journal. The Society for Nonprofit Organizations, 6314 Odana Road, Suite 1, Madison, WI 53719. 1-800-424-7367.

Comes with membership in the Society. It includes articles on computerization of office procedures and database systems.

On-Line. 462 Danbury Road, Wilton, CT 06897-2126. 1-203-761-1466. $99 per year for six issues.

Practical articles cover many subjects with tips on using databases from various vendors.

Orenstein, Glenn S. and Ruth M. Orenstein. *CompuServe Companion: Finding Newspapers and Magazines Online.* BiblioData, Box 61, Needham Heights, MA 02194, 1-617-444-1154. 1994. $29.95.

The book serves as a road map to the thousands of full text periodicals on CompuServe, directing users to get what is needed at the lowest cost. Provides online searching tips.

Rugge, Sue and Alfred Glossbrenner. *The Information Broker's Handbook,* 2nd ed. McGraw-Hill, $29.95.

It's written for those wanting a career as an information broker but it gives good advice about online searching and includes a disk with essential forms and sample letters.

Searcher: The Magazine for Database Professionals, Information Today, Inc., 143 Old Marlton Pike, Medford, NJ 08055-8750. 1-609-654-6266. $52.50 per year for ten issues.

Evaluates and describes electronic databases and products with searching tips and techniques.

Sherman, Tom. *Electronic Networking for Nonprofits: A Guide to Getting Started.* 1991. Benton Foundation, 1634 Eye Street, NW, 12th Floor, Washington, DC 20006. 1-202-638-5770. $7.00.

Tells how nonprofits can use the new technologies to establish and use networking to improve communications with other organizations and to get or provide information online.

Stoll, Clifford. *Silicon Snake Oil: Second Thoughts on the Information Highway.* Doubleday/Anchor. 1995. $14.00 pap.

Stoll says the Internet is not everything to everyone. He recommends person-to-person communications instead.

"Using DIALOG in the Development Office: Techniques, Databases, and Approaches for Utilizing Online Resources for Resource Development." 1992. Unpublished, but available from DIALOG. 1-800-334-2564

Very useful for most nonprofit offices that use DIALOG as a main online service.

ORGANIZATIONS AND FOUNDATIONS

Many groups are involved in making electronic technology available for use by nonprofit organizations. Here are examples.

Alliance for a Global Community
InterAction - Suite 801
1717 Massachusetts Avenue NW
Washington, DC 20036
1-202-667-8227
E-Mail: ia@interaction.org
http://www.vita.org/iaction/iaction.html

Realizing the Internet and other new information technologies have amazing power, this group is working to harness that power to assist humanitarian aid throughout the world. The Alliance is the communications and education program of Inter-Action, a coalition working to build public support for the developing world.

Association of Professional Researchers for Advancement
414 Plaza Drive, Suite 209
Westmont, IL 60559
1-708-655-0177
E-Mail: apra@adminsys.com

Formerly the American Prospect Research Association, this organization promotes and gives information about research in nonprofit organizations. Its annual conference and regional chapter meetings stress using the new technologies for research and networking.

Benton Foundation
1634 Eye Streeet NW, 12th Floor
Washington, DC 20006
1-202-638-5770
E-Mail: info-benton@cdinet.com
http://cdinet.com/benton/

The Benton Foundation provided leadership and tools to strengthen the communications capacities of nonprofit organizations. The foundation wishes to gain an effective voice for social change using the new technologies in the public interest. A foundation report, *What's Working Now,* gives examples of efficient technology use.

The Center for Media Education
1511 K Street NW, Suite 518
Washington, DC 20005
   1-202-628-2620
   E-Mail: cme@access.digex.net

The Center is dedicated to educating the public about critical media policy issues. One of its purposes is to promote fair and inexpensive access to electronic resources available on the information infrastructure. It gives useful information about access to the information superhighway and other electronic devices and publishes *infoActive* (previously listed.)

Center for Strategic Communications
505 Eighth Street, Suite 2000
New York, NY 10018-6505
   1-212-967-2843

This nonprofit organization informs and educates nonprofit managers about how to take advantage of the evolving communication environment.

CompuMentor
89 Stillman Street
San Francisco, CA 94107-1309
   1-800-659-3579
   E-Mail: cmentor@well.com

CompuMentor was formed in 1986 as a network of computer experts who wished to help nonprofit organizations join the computer age. Their publication, *CompuMentoring! Helping People Use Computers to Make a Difference,* explains their mission. Call for additional information.

Council for Advancement and Support of Education (CASE)
11 Dupont Circle, Suite 400
Washington, DC 20036
   1-202-328-5900

CASE sponsors workshops and seminars promoting development in education including prospect research with discussion on using computers for research.

Council on Foundations
1828 L Street NW
Washington, DC 20036-5168
 1-202-466-6512
 http://www.cof.org

This association of foundations deals with many of the current issues they face. One goal of the Council is to help foundations make information available with new types of technology. The Council publishes *Foundation News & Commentary*.

Electronic Frontier Foundation
1550 Bryant, Suite 725
San Francisco, CA 94103
 1-415-668-7171
 E-Mail: eff@eff.org
 http://www.eff.org

The foundation promotes use of technology by nonprofits.

Internet Nonprofit Center
738 Union Street
Brooklyn, NY 11215
 1-718-399-9224
 E-Mail: clandesm@panix.com
 http://www.human.com/inc/

This center seeks to provide information on more nonprofits than any other site in the world. It it sponsored by the American Institute of Philanthropy and aims to help individual donors and volunteers find out about and evaluate organizations. It also gives information on giving to nonprofits.

National Society of Fund Raising Executives
1101 King Street, Suite 700
Alexandria, VA 22314
 1-703-684-0410

This association realizes that computers and computerization are an important part of the work of a fund raiser. The NSFRE publishes *Advancing Philanthropy.*

Society for Nonprofit Organizations
6314 Odana Road
Madison, WI 53719
   1-608-274-9777

Using electronics for nonprofit management and research is a topic of interest to this society. It publishes *Nonprofit World.*

Telecommunications Cooperative Network
2101 Wilson Blvd, Suite 417
Arlington, VA 22201
   1-800-669-4826
   E-Mail: tcnhelp@tcn.org

This group assists nonprofits with consulting and training in the use of networking.

Vita - Volunteers in Technical Assistance
1600 Wilson Boulevard, Suite 500
Arlington, VA 22209
   1-703-276-1800
   E-Mail: vita@gmuvax.gmu.edu
   http://www.vita.org

VITA provides technical support as a leader in assisting information management, offering inexpensive communications systems, and providing access to electronic mail for those working in developing countries. It is affiliated with InterAction and the Alliance for a Global Community in the publication of *The Essential Internet: Basics for NGOS.*

Index

~

Hill, Lance, 192
Hilts, Paul, 172
Hispanic Magazine, 208
Hispanic Web sites, 207-208
Historical Stock/Fund Pricing, 116
Home Office Computing, 102
Home pages, 151, 159-161, 192-200
Hoover's Business Resources, 132
Hoover's Company Database, 28, 108
Hoover's Handbook Web site, 205
Hoover's Masterlist of Major U.S. Companies, 28
HTML (HyperText Markup Language), 152
HTTP (HyperText Transfer Protocol), 152

~

Idaho, University, "Grant Getter's Guide to the Internet," 195
IDI Valley Technologies, 36
Illinois, University / Champaign-Urbana, 153
Impact Online, 193
Index to Legal Periodicals, 124
infoActive, 55, 142, 237-238, 242
Information Access Company, 43, 46, 51
Information America, 101
Information Please Business Almanac, 109
Information Please General Almanac, 109
Information Today, Inc., 19, 238, 240
Information USA, 126
InfoTrac, 43-44
"Inside owners," 24

Insider Trading Monitor, 69
Institute for Global Communications, 141, 198
Institute for Nonprofit Organization Management, survey, 56
InterAction, 198, 244
Internal Revenue Service, 195, 211
International fund raisers listserv, 180
International Stocks Database, 124
Internet, 143-161, 187-200, 201-223
    access on CompuServe, 127
    access on America Online, 135
    access on Microsoft Network, 137
    access on Prodigy, 136
    access on Genie, 137-138
    charges, 157-159
    connecting, 157-159
    e-mail, 162-171
    equipment, 157-158
    error messages, 156
    etiquette, 185
    grants, 194-196
    history, 147-149, 188
    listservs, 172-186
    search engines, 188-191
    smileys, 185
    terminology, 149-155
    traffic jams, 155-156
Internet Nonprofit Center, 197, 243
Internet Prospector, 191, 218, 219
"Internet Resources for Non-Profit Service Organizations," 193
IQUEST, 120-124
Issues Forum on CompuServe, 127

~